Rajasthan on a Platter

Rajasthan on a Platter

Healthy · Tasty · Easy

Suman Bhatnagar
Pushpa Gupta

NIYOGI BOOKS

Published by

NIYOGI BOOKS

D-78, Okhla Industrial Area, Phase-I
New Delhi-110 020, INDIA
Tel: 91-11-26816301, 49327000
Fax: 91-11-26810483, 26813830
Email: niyogibooks@gmail.com
Website: www.niyogibooksindia.com

Text © Suman Bhatnagar & Pushpa Gupta
Photographs © Amit Gupta

Editor: Mohua Mitra
Design: Nabanita Das

ISBN: 978-93-85285-11-0
Publication: 2015

Printed at: Niyogi Offset Pvt. Ltd.,
New Delhi, India

This book is for
our mothers who
inculcated in us the love
for cooking and for our
grandchildren to carry
the tradition forward

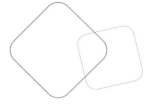

Photo courtesy: Sanjay Vishwakarma

RHYTHM OF LIFE: Colourful performance of the popular folk dance drama Gavari by the Bhils in Thoor ki Pal—a village near Udaipur

Pg 2: GANGAUR FESTIVAL: A procession with Gangaur Mata

Pg 4-5: BEAUTY AND SERENITY: View from Amber fort

Contents

Foreword **11**

Preface **13**

Welcome to Rajasthan and the Local
Cuisine (Padharo Mahre Desh) **15**

Flavours of Cereals (Zaika Anaj Ka) **25**
Wheat 27
Sadi bati **29**
Churma **31**
Dupper **32**
Missi roti **33**
Gulgule **34**
Lapsi **35**
Daal dhokli **36**
Wheat ghughari **38**
Wheat flour roti **39**
Puri **40**

Plain paratha **41**
Bharwa / aloo paratha **42**
Sabzi paratha **43**
Meetha paratha **44**
Halwa **45**
Doodh dalia **46**
Maize 47
Maize roti **48**
Makki ka dhokla **49**
Raab **51**
Maize papadi / khichiya **53**
Bhutta pakodi **57**
Bhutta sabzi **59**
Bhutta pulav **61**
Jajaria **63**
Bhutta barfi **65**
Bajra 67
Bajra kheech **69**
Bajra gudmudia **71**
Bajra khichada **72**

Power of Pulses (Damdaar Daalen) **73**
Mixed daal **75**
Mangodi / badi **76**
Mangodi ki sabzi **77**
Kadhi pakodi **78**
Pakodi sabzi **80**
Besan gatte **81**
Sabut moth **83**
Besan chakki **85**

Vegetables in a Variety (Sabziyan Swaad-bhari) **87**
Ratalu sabzi **89**
Bharwa besan mirch **91**
Mirchi bada **93**
Kachha kela chhilka sabzi **95**
Dried vegetables curry **96**
Pach kuta / ker sangri **98**
Meethi dana methi sabzi **99**
Dana methi papad **100**
Lahsan chutney **102**
Papad sabzi **104**
Kachhi haldi ki sabzi **105**
Mirchi ke tapore **106**

Meat, Poultry, Eggs (Maansahaari Zaika) **107**
Laal maans **108**
Keema matar **110**
Chicken curry **111**
Egg curry **112**
Fish curry **114**
Fish fry (snack/ starter) **116**

Festive Fare (Khana Teej
          Tyoharon Ka) **117**
Til laddoo **119**
Til barfi **121**
Dudhiya kheech **122**
Kesaria bhaat **124**
Oliya 125
Namkeen oliya **126**
Meethi oliya **128**
Papadi 129
Meethi papadi **130**
Namkeen besan papadi **131**
Rabdi ke malpua **133**
Roth **134**
Guna **136**

Glossary **138**
Appendix **140**
Table of Measures **145**
Acknowledgements **147**
Index **148**

The people are friendly and full of joy; the vibrant colours of their clothes and their home décor spread a rare cheer

The majestic forts and palaces are the body of Rajasthan; folk music its soul. And the lip smacking regional cuisine adds to the charm, making it an irresistible treat for the senses

A.S.M.

Foreword

I wish to congratulate the two learned Professors of Maharana Pratap University of Agriculture and Technology, Udaipur, Rajasthan—Dr. Suman Bhatnagar and Dr. Pushpa Gupta for their publication titled *Rajasthan on a Platter: Healthy, Tasty, Easy.* The publication is a testimony to their deep interest and decades of experience in teaching and researching issues concerning cuisine and nutrition with a focus on our state of Rajasthan.

The entire subject of cuisine, and the authenticity of its ingredients and cooking techniques, is one that is close to my heart. I have always taken a personal interest in our kitchens. I also spend considerable time preparing a variety of dishes at my private residence. I find cooking not only very therapeutic but it is also a continuous enjoyable learning experience for me.

Food that is cooked with care and love has a distinct taste of its own. Every chef realizes this truism and I am happy to note that Dr. Suman and Dr. Pushpa have emphasized the importance of hygiene, nutrition and low-fire cooking as they have researched and written this publication for today's generation.

Rajasthan, I have mentioned it time and again, has much to contribute to the modern world in terms of its intangible cultural heritage. While our state is famous for its palaces, forts and temples, it cannot be only identified with this tangible heritage. Cuisine, as the reader shall discover in the following pages, reflects the rich biodiversity of our state and it is a fine example of our 'living heritage'. Every home - be it of a farmer in the rural areas or of an urban professional - is a repository of this intangible cultural heritage. We need to be constantly on alert that these culinary practices and traditional techniques, are not lost over time, nor ignored or defaced by people today.

On our part in Udaipur, and from The City Palace, we continue to work towards the preservation of the 'living heritage' of Mewar. We are serving society and shouldering the moral responsibilities bequeathed to us as the legacy of the Custodians of Mewar.

Our endeavour is to reaffirm Udaipur as a 'centre of excellence' and a seat of learning. Dr. Suman Bhatnagar and Dr. Pushpa Gupta's publication is a laudable step in this direction. Niyogi Books deserves praise for their support to the authors and their commitment to promoting India's culinary heritage.

Arvind Singh Mewar

Preface

Rajasthan is the largest state of India and constitutes 5.67% of the country's population. It has 33 districts with different agro-climatic zones. The region's indigenous food items like certain kinds of cereals, pulses, vegetables and fruits, as well as oil seeds and milk are produced in different zones and are usually consumed by the local population residing in that particular region of the state. Rajasthanis honour tradition—the realms of food, clothing, culture, social and religious customs and practices continue more or less as per age-old tradition. So people prefer to eat familiar home food, prepared in the traditional home kitchen and generally do not exchange regional variations of culinary traditions even within the different agro-climatic zones of the state. *Bhujia, namkeen* and *papad*—the *daal* or *besan*-based dry snacks of Rajasthan are popular all over India and abroad. The Rajasthani people have a sweet tooth, hence fresh supplies of a variety of *mithai*s (sweets) is available in every city and village in the state.

Rajasthan offers a wide and a most delectable variety of traditional food items, which are unique in taste and add plenty of nutritive value to the diet. Gradually, with the fast-changing scenario and life increasingly shifting to the fast track, some of these traditional dishes are losing out to the global fast food culture and getting lost in this transition. Hours of toil in the kitchen to lay a meal for the family on the table is not of top priority any longer as work hours outside home have increased and the younger generation has adapted itself to multi-tasking and being 'on the job' and 'on call' almost through the entire day. Eating habits, along with lifestyle, have also undergone a change; with limited time on hand 'snacking' is increasingly replacing full sit-down meals while 'finger food' and 'quick bites' during a social engagement in the evening often serve the purpose of a light dinner.

It is therefore with this thought in mind that we have embarked upon the project of writing a book on some of the select homemade traditional recipes—simply to transfer the home-grown knowledge to the young generation of Rajasthan as well as the people of other states and countries. We hope that these dishes and recipes will be popular among future generations of cooks, homemakers and food connoisseurs.

The select recipes are grouped in five categories—cereals, pulses, vegetables, non-vegetarian dishes and special dishes for festivals. There are different ways of cooking the same dish but we have consciously tried to present the simplest method in this book. Each recipe is standardised for calculating preparation time, cooking time, ingredients, nutritional value and its variations. Each recipe has been combined with different food items chosen thoughtfully to present the concept of a tasty and nutritious meal. The book also provides information on the recommended nutritional allowances for different types of people—men and women with sedentary as well as fast lifestyles, with moderate to heavy work schedules and children in various age groups. One can roughly form an idea of the amount of food one may consume to meet the required daily intake of dietary nutrients.

The book contains select traditional recipes of Rajasthan. The recipes have been standardised. Nutritive values of the recipes have been minutely calculated, based on research and reference of the book *Nutritive Value of Indian Foods* by C. Gopalan and others, published by the National Institute of Nutrition, Hyderabad 2011, in particular. Preparation and cooking time for each recipe has been estimated. The various food combinations necessary to present a meal, value addition and interesting but healthy variations in recipes have been thoughtfully incorporated. The recommended dietary daily allowance for each group men, women and children has been provided so that one can get a rough idea of the daily intake of nutrients and calories. It is hoped that the younger generation of homemakers, chefs and food lovers will try out some of these recipes in their state-of-the-art modular kitchens and relish the traditional Rajasthani *zaika* (flavours).

Suman Bhatnagar
Pushpa Gupta

Welcome to Rajasthan and the Local Cuisine

Padharo Mahre Desh

Rajasthan is located in the north-western part of the subcontinent. It is bounded in the north and north east by the states of Punjab and Haryana, in the east and south east by the states of Uttar Pradesh and Madhya Pradesh, in the south west by the state of Gujarat and to the west and north west by Pakistan. The total area of the state is 3,42,239 sq km. Jaipur is the capital and located in the east central part of the state.

Rajasthan is a land of romance, royalty, valour and chivalry. It is one of the most beautiful states with the Thar desert in the west, the mighty Aravalli ranges in the south and lush green fields in the northern and eastern parts. The scorching desert gently merges into lush green deciduous forests. There are several wildlife sanctuaries and national parks in the state. Tourism contributes largely to the state economy as Rajasthan is one of the famous tourist attractions in the country and the world.

The Thar desert is the world's eighteenth largest subtropical desert and is famed as the most populated desert in the world. The sun-kissed golden sand dunes and miles of the golden Thar in Jaisalmer, the shimmering, beautiful lakes in Udaipur and Mount Abu, deep emerald forests rich in a wide variety of flora and fauna – including the majestic Royal Bengal tiger – the imposing Aravalli ranges and magnificent old forts, palaces, sculptured temples and other monuments add to the unique beauty of the state's landscape and make it one of the most picturesque, colourful and tourist-friendly regions in India. Famous rivers—the Beas, Chambal, Banas, Luni and Mahi form

Pg 15: BIRD'S-EYE VIEW: The mighty Aravalli ranges encircling towns and cities

Right: GREEN AND GOLD: The scorching desert gently merges into lush green deciduous forests

Photo courtesy (p. 15 & above): Arti Sharma

the life lines of the state. The old palaces of Jaipur, Jodhpur, Jaisalmer, Deeg and Udaipur tell the magnificent stories of the royals. Amer, Chittorgarh, Jaisalmer, Ranthambhore, Gagaron (Jhalawar) and Kumbhalgarh forts stand as witness to the famed chivalry of maharajas and maharanas of the Rajputana region. Some of these forts have been declared world heritage sites by UNESCO.

At the time of India's Independence there were a number of princely states in the country. The present state of Rajasthan was established in 1956. At present there are 33 administrative districts and 25 parliamentary constituencies. There are eight different regions (*anchals*), among them Haroti, Marwar, Mewar, Shekhawati, Doondhar, Mewat, Brij and Wagad, based on the local socio-cultural traditions and regional language/ dialect popularly spoken in that particular area. Rajasthan celebrates nature and the changes in season through its countless festivals and fairs. The people need little reason to celebrate or hold festivals; a turn of the season or a wedding in the family or neighbourhood rings in

Right: TRADITION AND RITUAL: Gangaur festival in all its splendour

joyous celebration marked by popular and folk rituals, music, dancing and feasting. People are fond of bright colours and prefer to wear colourful dresses to beat the monotonous expanse of a somewhat harsh, semi-arid natural environment in many parts of the state.

The state boasts a 5000-year-old cultural tradition. The state is known for its rich aesthetic and cultural traditions which are essentially a part and soul of an Indian way of living steeped in age-old customs, beliefs and ancient values. Rajasthan is a rich mosaic of Indian heritage, subtly infused and enriched with cultural and social diversity accumulated down the ages as well as with contemporary global influences. Folk songs

CELEBRATING LIFE: With Gair—a folk dance enlivened with bright colours, traditional costume and lively music and dances are a vital part of Rajasthani culture. Here tradition blends seamlessly with the modern and the contemporary, resonating exuberance, vibrant colours and a rare warmth. Most of the old palaces, the havelis where maharajas lived, have now been developed and converted into famous luxury hotels. Some of the world's famous temples and mosques in the state attract thousands of pilgrims through the year. The people of Rajasthan freely practise their individual faiths and live in perfect harmony with each other. The rich old heritage of the state attracts national and international tourists.

There are different agro-climatic conditions associated with harsh natural environment. The high temperature in summer and frosty cold nights of winter are well-known. The water scarcity and the sandy and hilly, rocky terrain make it difficult to cultivate different crops, especially vegetables and fruits. However the hard working people of the state grow cereals, pulses, vegetables, spices, oilseeds and produce milk to fulfill their own requirement. Some of the products like spices, oilseeds and milk are sold in the other states. As a result of improved transport facilities and

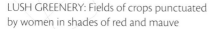

LUSH GREENERY: Fields of crops punctuated by women in shades of red and mauve

increasingly better roads, other varieties of vegetables and fruits from the neighbouring states are easily transported to supplement the demand in the urban areas of Rajasthan.

Rajasthan has a rich tradition of cuisines, for this land had some of the finest cooks in the royal palaces. The food in Rajasthan is as diverse as the topography of the state. The people are friendly and full of joy; the vibrant colours of their clothes and in their home décor spread a rare cheer. The people are famous for their *manuhar* (hospitality). Rajasthani cuisine is spicy, rich in fat and *meetha* (sweet). Spices like *heeng, jeera, ajwain, lal mirch. saunf, methi dana* (see glossary for English names), ginger, garlic and onion find a special place in the cuisine and add flavour, aroma and some medicinal value to the food. A variety of recipes in different parts of the state is prepared from the main crops grown in the respective regions. Rajasthan state is high on milk production. Milk and a range of milk products like buttermilk, curd, ghee, paneer and *khoya* are used in plenty in the Rajasthani kitchen, which provide protein, calcium and vitamins. The western part of the state partially fulfills the total milk demand in Delhi and the National Capital Region (NCR).

Wheat is consumed in the entire state through the year. Maize dishes are specially prepared in the southern part while bajra (pearl millet) dishes are enjoyed in the western and eastern parts during winter. Consumption of vegetables and fruits is limited as these are grown where irrigation facility

GLASS BANGLES ON SALE: Colour and glitter amidst the desert monochrome bring joy and vibrancy

is available. Ker sangri, daal bati churma, gatte ke sabzi, jhakolma puri and lal maans are very popular dishes in Rajasthan. The people of Rajasthan have a pronounced sweet tooth. Thus sweets form an important part of the day's menu and halwai shops line the streets and alleys of Rajasthan. The mawa kachori of Jodhpur, ghewar of Jaipur, Alwar pak of Alwar, dil jani of Udaipur and rasgullas of Bikaner are some of the popular regional delicacies. Special food is enjoyed during different festivals, adding variety to the daily home meals. The traditional food items of Rajasthan presented in this book fulfill the

FESTIVE TIMES: The famous halwais of
Rajasthan making and selling savouries
and sweets

nutritional needs of people of all age groups and therefore a family with members representing
three generations can live a perfectly healthy and reasonably active life, cooking and eating these
traditional home dishes at all meals.

However, with passage of time, globalisation of the Indian market and changing lifestyles,
traditional food is gradually disappearing from the Rajasthani kitchen. Rajasthani food is also
not so readily available at fast food joints and regular restaurants—like the dosa, idli and other
traditional specialities of South India. On the other hand fast food is gradually capturing the
dining tables of city homes. It is common knowledge that fast food does not promote good
health. Hence an effort has been made to disseminate the knowledge and step up the popularity
of traditional and nutritious Rajasthani food among youngsters through this book.

Flavours of
Cereals

Zaika Anaj Ka

The major cereal crops in Rajasthan are wheat, bajra, maize, sorghum and barley. Paddy is also cultivated in command areas[1]. Wheat is mostly grown in the northern and eastern parts of the state where irrigation facilities are available during the Rabi season (for winter crops harvested in spring). Maize, bajra and jowar are Kharif crops (monsoon crops harvested in autumn) and being normally rain-fed, are not dependent on irrigation. Maize is cultivated in the southern part of the state while bajra and jowar in the western and eastern parts of the state.

Wheat and jowar are consumed generally during summer while maize and bajra are consumed in the winter season. These cereals are a good, natural source of carbohydrates, vitamin B complex, minerals and roughage. The nutritive value of cereals commonly consumed in Rajasthan is given in Appendix Table[1].

Cereals in Rajasthan are consumed in different forms and combinations. The concept of combination food has gained new heights and

STAPLE CEREAL: Crops before harvest

exclusivity in Rajasthan. Preparation methods of cereals – wheat, maize and bajra – are given in the following section.

---

1   Command areas: An area which can be irrigated under an economically viable scheme and be made cultivable.

Wheat

A large variety of dishes are prepared from wheat and
included in the daily diet of people in Rajasthan; there are
some earmarked for special occasions and festivals too. A
few of the basic wheat-based recipes consumed daily in
most Indian homes, like the regular roti, paratha, puri and
dalia have also been presented here along with the special
delicacies, for the benefit of beginners in the kitchen and
those who are not regular consumers of wheat-based
Indian meals but would like to try their hand at some of
these daily delicacies of Rajasthani homes.

Bati: Rajasthan is famous for daal, bati and churma. This is a traditional and a popular combination across the state. Bati is a wheat flour ball, baked/ roasted/ boiled/ fried and dipped in pure ghee. Bati is served with mixed daal. Churma laddoos are made from wheat flour, ghee and sugar. The combination produces a mixed and exciting punch of salt-sweet-chilli flavours tempered by desi ghee and also a unique combined texture of crunchy solids with soft solids and viscous fluids. This diet is relished at picnics as well as religious functions and special occasions.

$\mathcal{S}$adi bati
Baked balls of wheat flour

makes **8 batis**
preparation time **20 minutes**
cooking time **25 minutes**

Ingredients
Wheat • 250g
Ghee • 80g (40g for moyan
   and 40g for serving)
Salt • to taste
Water • for making dough

Method
- Take wheat flour in a thali, mix salt and ghee. Rub in and knead the flour well. Prepare semi-hard dough. Keep it covered with cloth for an hour. Make medium-sized balls.
- Heat an oven to 180°c or a gas tandoor. Arrange batis in tray or on tandoor grill.
- Bake on medium gas flame. Change sides of bati 2 to 3 times till it turns golden. The process is over and the batis done when thin cracks appear on the surface of the batis while baking.
- Remove from tandoor. Crack bati and pour a few drops of warm ghee in it.
- Serve hot with daal.

Value addition

Bengal gram daal flour (besan), semolina (rava/ sooji), fennel (saunf), coarsely ground coriander seeds (coarse dhania), carom (ajwain) and a pinch of turmeric (haldi) can be added to the wheat flour.

Bati made of maize flour is common in southern Rajasthan.

Variations

- **Bafla Bati**-The wheat flour balls are boiled in water for 15 to 20 minutes on high flame. When balls come up to the surface, these are removed from water and are allowed to dry. Thereafter these are baked the same way as sadi bati.
- **Talwan Bati**-After boiling the balls, they are dried and then deep fried in ghee.
- **Stuffed Bati**-For the stuffing, prepare a masala (spicy) filling of boiled potatoes, peas, green chillies, coriander leaves and dry masala. Take a dough ball and press with fingers. Now fill it with the masala stuffing and close the opening properly. These are then baked or fried.

Nutritive value

Protein g	Energy kcal	Calcium mg	Iron mg	Carotene µg	Thiamin (B1) mg	Riboflavin (B2) mg	Niacin (B3) mg
30.3	1527	120	12.3	557	1.2	0.4	10.8

Churma is a traditional Rajasthani sweet dish and it is generally enjoyed with daal and baati. It is also prepared as a festival sweet on Ganesh Chaturthi.

makes **10 to 12 laddoos**
preparation time **30 minutes**
cooking time **30 minutes**

*C*hurma
Wheat flour sweet balls

Ingredients
Coarse wheat flour • 250g
Sugar powder • 200g
Ghee • 180g
Coconut powder • 15g
Almonds (chopped) • 10g
Water • for making dough

Method
- Add 60g of ghee as moyan in the flour, rub well, prepare semi-hard dough.
- Make muthias (fist-sized balls) and deep fry till golden brown.
- Break these muthias when hot and grind into coarse powder.
- Add remaining ghee, sugar, coconut powder and chopped almonds in the coarse powder.
- Make laddoos of the mixture when it is hot.
- Serve with daal and baati.

Value addition
- Suji/ rice flour/ maize flour/ bajra flour can be used to make churma.
- Dried rose petals can be added to churma.
- Instead of deep frying the muthias, thick rotis can be baked for making churma.

Nutritive value

Protein g	Energy kcal	Calcium mg	Iron mg	Carotene µg	Thiamin (B1) mg	Riboflavin (B2) mg	Niacin (B3) mg
32.3	3334	150	14	1240	1.1	0.4	14.2

 Dupper
Roti with two layers

makes **10 duppers/ 20 layers**
preparation time **10 minutes**
cooking time **15 minutes**

Ingredients
Wheat flour • 250g
Ghee • 15g
Salt • to taste
Water • for making dough

Method
- Add salt in flour, make soft dough and keep it for half an hour.
- Divide the dough in twenty parts and make balls.
- Roll out each ball of about 2" in diameter.
- Apply oil on one roll and keep another roll over it. Now roll it out in a full size roti.
- Put it on a hot tawa and bake it from both the sides.
- Separate two layers. Since oil has been applied between two layers, it is easy to separate. Apply ghee on both layers. These layers are very thin and soft.

Combination
Hot duppers are enjoyed with daal, sabzi or aam ras (mango juice).

Variation
- Same dough can be used for making chapati/ roti, puri, plain or stuffed paratha.

Nutritive value

Protein g	Energy kcal	Calcium mg	Iron mg	Carotene µg	Thiamin (B1) mg	Riboflavin (B2) mg	Niacin (B3) mg
30.3	987	120	12.3	167	1.2	0.4	10.8

Missi roti
Bejad roti

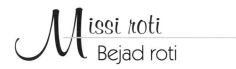

makes **4 rotis**
preparation time **10 minutes**
cooking time **15 minutes**

Missi roti is more nutritious because it is a mix of cereals and pulses. Wheat, barley and whole chana are mixed in the proportion of 1.5:1:1. It is milled into fine flour and sifted to take out bran especially of the barley and the chana. Proportion of mixing these grains can vary. Flour can be stored in a cool dry place for weeks and months.

Ingredients

Missi flour • 175g
Ghee • 20g
Salt • to taste
Water • for making dough

Method

- Take out missi flour in a parat (large round flat metal plate with raised edges and a wide surface for preparing dough); add salt.
- Prepare dough by adding water and keep it for ½ hour.
- Knead well. Roll out roti and bake from both sides on a hot tawa.
- Apply ghee on one side and serve hot.

Value addition

- Finely chopped leafy vegetables can be added in the flour while preparing the dough.

Nutritive value

Protein g	Energy kcal	Calcium mg	Iron mg	Carotene µg	Thiamin B1 mg	Riboflavin B2 mg	Niacin B3 mg
23.2	800	144	6.2	182.5	0.7	0.3	6.9

Gulgule
Fried sweet balls

makes **30 to 35 pieces**
preparation time **10 minutes**
cooking time **10 minutes**

Ingredients
Wheat flour • 250g
Sugar/ jaggery • 200g
Fennel seeds (saunf) • 10g
Khuskhus (poppy seeds) • 10g
Water • for making batter
Oil • for frying

Method
- Take wheat flour in a bowl, mix saunf (fennel), poppy seeds and mix well.
- Dissolve sugar/ jaggery in water. Make a batter of medium consistency by adding sugar/ jaggery water slowly in the flour while mixing well. Avoid lump formation. Add plain water if needed. Keep batter for ½ an hour.
- Fry small balls in hot ghee on medium flame till they turn golden.
- Gulgules can be served with chutney or curd or even without condiments.

Value addition and variation
- Addition of til in the flour makes it crispy.
- Gulgule can be made from bajra flour.
- Same batter with a slightly thinner consistency can be used for making cheela (pan cakes)

Nutritive value

Protein g	Energy kcal	Calcium mg	Iron mg	Carotene µg	Thiamin B1 mg	Riboflavin B2 mg	Niacin B3 mg
32.5	2293	280	1705	635	1.2	0.4	10.8

$\mathcal{L}$apsi
Dessert

Lapsi is prepared on festivals or on auspicious occasions and is offered as *prashaad* to the deity.

makes **4 bowls**
preparation time **5 minutes**
cooking time **20 minutes**

Ingredients
Wheat dalia ∘ 100g
Sugar/ jaggery ∘ 80g
Ghee ∘ 20g
Badam (almonds) ∘ 10g
Kishmish (raisins) ∘ 5g
Cardamom (elayichi)
   powder ground from
   ∘ 2–3 pieces
Water ∘ 250ml

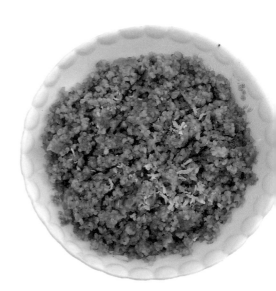

Method
- Heat ghee in a pan, sauté dalia till it turns golden in colour.
- Add water. Stir well. Cook dalia on high flame and let it stay on for 2-3 boils. Lower the flame, cover the pan and cook till it is done. Stir it at intervals to avoid the contents sticking to the pan.
- Add sugar/ jaggery and mix well. Cook for another five minutes on slow flame.
- Add chopped almonds, cardamom powder and raisins. Serve hot.

Combination
Lapsi is enjoyed with kadhi and daal.

Nutritive Value

Protein g	Energy kcal	Calcium mg	Iron mg	Carotene µg	Thiamin (B1) mg	Riboflavin (B2) mg	Niacin (B3) mg
14.1	937	90	6.2	184	0.5	0.2	6.0

Daal dhokli
Spicy flour balls in lentil soup

makes **4 bowls**
preparation time **25 minutes**
cooking time **30 minutes**

Ingredients

for dhokli:
Wheat flour ○ 100g
Bengal gram daal (besan)
   flour ○ 25g
Ghee ○ 25g
Salt ○ to taste
Red chilli powder ○ 5g
Carom (ajwain) ○ a pinch

Cumin (jeera) powder ○ 3g
Cooking soda ○ a pinch
Water ○ for making dough
for daal:
Green gram daal (chhilka/with
   skin) ○ 40g
Bengal gram daal ○ 10g
Onion ○ 50g
Garlic ○ 3-4 cloves

Ginger ○ ½" piece
Coriander leaves ○ 3-4 stems
Ghee ○ 10g
Turmeric (haldi) powder ○ 5g
Red chilli powder ○ 5g
Salt ○ to taste
Water ○ 200ml

Method

- Wash the daals. Grind onion, garlic and ginger into fine paste.
- Heat ghee in pressure cooker, add the onion-ginger-garlic paste and sauté it. Add water, daals, dry spices and salt. Cook till pressure cooker steams up to one whistle (half done); remove from the gas stove.
- To prepare dhoklis, mix wheat flour and besan (Bengal gram daal flour). Add ghee and masala in the flour and rub well. Prepare soft dough and knead it well. Make small balls, press each ball between two palms. Add the dhoklis in the half-done daal. Cook on high flame till the liquid boils, reduce to slow flame and cook for 15 minutes.
- When the dhoklis begin to float in the daal it indicates that the dish is fully done.
- Temper the daal with asafoetida (heeng) and cumin (jeera) powder—warmed and spluttered separately in ghee. Garnish with finely cut coriander leaves.
- Serve immediately to retain heat and the flavour of the fresh temper.

Nutritive value

Protein g	Energy kcal	Calcium mg	Iron mg	Carotene µg	Thiamin (B1) mg	Riboflavin (B2) mg	Niacin (B3) mg
30.7	970	118.6	8.9	252	0.8	0.3	5.6

Wheat ghughari
Whole wheat savoury

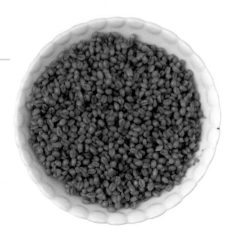

makes **4 bowls**
preparation time **5 minutes**
cooking time **30 minutes**

Ingredients

Whole wheat
  (debranned) • 100g
Oil • 10g
Onion • 30g
Tomato • 30g
Green chillies • 2
Coriander leaves • 3-4 stems
Salt and red chilli powder
  • to taste

Method

- Soak debranned wheat overnight. Cook grains in pressure cooker on high flame till one whistle. Lower the flame and cook for another 20 minutes. Open the cooker when cool.
- Finely chop onion, ginger, tomato, coriander leaves and green chillies.
- Heat oil in pan and sauté finely chopped ingredients for a minute. Add salt and ghughari in pan, mix well. Garnish with coriander leaves.
- Serve hot as a snack.

Variation

- Whole wheat is also used for making ghughari.
- Debranned maize and bajra are often used to make ghughari.
- Debranned cereals are available in market.

Note - Process of debranning at home has been described in the recipe for Bajra kheech.

Nutritive value

Protein g	Energy kcal	Calcium mg	Iron mg	Carotene µg	Thiamin (B1) mg	Riboflavin (B2) mg	Niacin (B3) mg
12.6	458	76.7	5.8	239	0.5	0.2	5.9

Wheat flour roti
Chapati

makes **5**
preparation time **10 minutes**
cooking time **10 minutes**

Ingredients

Flour ∘ 100g
Salt ∘ to taste
Ghee ∘ 10g
Water ∘ to make dough

Method

- Take flour in a parat. Add a pinch of salt. Mix well. Make medium soft dough by adding water gradually. Knead it well. Keep for half an hour.
- Divide the dough in five equal portions and make balls. Apply dry flour and roll each ball on rolling board and apply dry flour again once or twice to avoid the dough getting stuck on the rolling board and the pin. Roll it in a 5"-6" diameter round.
- Put it on hot tawa. Turn it over once and turn again when baked. Puff it with a clean cloth on tawa or put it on direct flame. Use tongs for turning or puffing roti.
- Apply ghee on one side and spread over the roti. Serve hot with daal, sabzi or kadhi.

Nutritive Value

Protein g	Energy kcal	Calcium mg	Iron mg	Carotene µg	Thiamin B1 mg	Riboflavin B2 mg	Niacin B3 mg
12.1	431	48	4.9	89	0.5	0.2	4.3

Puri
Fried wheat flour rounds

Puri is generally fried on special occasions or festivals. Puri-sabzi also makes a quick breakfast or midday meal.

makes **10**
preparation time **10 minutes**
cooking time **10 minutes**

Ingredients
Wheat flour ∘ 100g
Salt ∘ to taste
Oil ∘ for deep frying
Water ∘ to make dough

Method
* Take flour in a parat. Add salt and prepare dough. The dough should be slightly harder than the dough for roti.
* Divide the dough into ten equal parts. Make balls. Roll out each ball into 3"-3.5" diameter.
* Heat oil in kadai. Deep fry puri and ladle out when it swells into a ball and turns golden.
* Serve hot with sabzi.

Combination
Hot puris are enjoyed with raita, vegetable curries and fries, chutney, pickles and kheer.

Variation
* Add ajwain and one tea spoon oil while preparing dough to enhance taste.
* Puris can be a part of the main meal, as the base cereal dish. They can also be served as a snack.

Nutritive Value

Protein g	Energy kcal	Calcium mg	Iron mg	Carotene µg	Thiamin B1 mg	Riboflavin B2 mg	Niacin B3 mg
12.1	611	48	4.9	29	0.49	0.17	4.3

Plain paratha

makes **4**
preparation time **10 minutes**
cooking time **10 minutes**

Ingredients

Wheat flour ∘ 100g
Ghee ∘ 30g
Salt ∘ to taste
Water ∘ to prepare dough

Method

- Add salt in flour and prepare soft dough by adding water gradually. Keep it for ½ an hour.
- Divide dough in 4 equal parts and make balls. Roll out each ball into 2"-3" diameter. Apply oil and roll them out. Fold the rolled out dough balls to make half moons. Spread oil on them and fold again to make triangles. Dust dry flour on both sides and roll them out like rotis into 5" X 6" triangles.
- Shallow fry on hot tawa by turning sides. Apply oil or ghee on both sides while being fried. Remove from tawa when the triangle turns golden brown.
- Serve hot with sabzi or mutton/ chicken keema curry.

Nutritive Value

Protein g	Energy kcal	Calcium mg	Iron mg	Carotene µg	Thiamin B1 mg	Riboflavin B2 mg	Niacin B3 mg
12.1	701	48	4.9	29	0.49	0.17	4.3

Bharwa / aloo paratha
Stuffed paratha

makes **4**
preparation time **15 minutes**
cooking time **10 minutes**

Ingredients

Wheat flour • 100g
Potato • 100g
Ghee • 40g (oil can
   also be used)
Water • to make dough
Dry masala – salt, red chilli
   powder, fennel (saunf)

crushed, cumin (jeera)
powder, dry mango
(amchur) powder, garam
masala powder • to taste
Green masala – 1-2 finely
chopped green chillies,
grated ginger ½", coriander
leaves – 2-3 stems

Method

- Prepare dough like the roti dough by adding water gradually, press and knead till soft and keep it standing for ½ an hour.
- Divide the dough in 4 equal parts and make balls.
- Roll out ball into a disc of 3" diameter. Put one table spoon of stuffing in the centre of the roll. Close the roll nicely by pressing the opening firmly with the help of fingers. Flatten the ball with the help of your palm. Dust flour on it and roll it out into 5"-6" diameter.
- Shallow fry it on a hot tawa by applying oil or ghee on both sides. Remove when it turns golden brown.
- Serve hot with chutney, pickle or curd.

Variation

- Boiled mashed potato + boiled peas/ grated radish/ grated carrot/ grated cauliflower/ grated paneer can be used for the stuffing. Boiled moong, and urad daal with dry and green masala can also be stuffed into the paratha.

Nutritive Value

Protein g	Energy kcal	Calcium mg	Iron mg	Carotene µg	Thiamin B1 mg	Riboflavin B2 mg	Niacin B3 mg	Vit. C
13.7	798	67.2	5.58	408	0.59	0.18	5.5	28.7

$\mathcal{S}$abzi paratha
Vegetable paratha

makes **4**
preparation time **10 minutes**
cooking time **10 minutes**

Ingredients

Wheat flour ∘ 100g
Besan (Bengal gram daal flour)
  ∘ 20g
Salt ∘ a pinch
Coarsely ground fennel
  (saunf) ∘ 2g
Oil ∘ 10g (for moyan)
Oil for shallow frying ∘ 40g
Chopped collard greens ∘ 30g
  (methi/ palak/ bathua)

Water ∘ to prepare dough
Dry masala – salt, red chilli
  powder, crushed fennel,
  cumin powder, dry mango
  (amchur) powder, garam
  masala powder ∘ to taste
Green masala – finely
  chopped green chillies – 1-2
  pieces, grated ginger – ½"
  coriander leaves – 2-3 stems

Method

- Mix flour, besan (Bengal gram daal flour), dry masala. Add oil for moyan and mix it well. Add finely chopped leafy vegetable and green masala. Prepare hard dough by adding water gradually. Keep it standing for 10-15 minutes.
- Divide dough in 4 parts and make balls. Roll out each ball into 5"-6" diameter discs.
- Shallow fry the paratha on medium flame by applying oil on both sides. Remove when it turns golden-brown.
- Serve hot with chutney, curd or pickle with a blob of butter melting on top (optional).

Variation

- Puris can be prepared with this dough and served as a tasty snack.

Nutritive Value

Protein g	Energy kcal	Calcium mg	Iron mg	Carotene µg	Thiamin B1 mg	Riboflavin B2 mg	Niacin B3 mg	Vit. C
17.3	881	187.2	6.7	1112	0.59	0.27	5.1	21.8

Meetha paratha
Sweet paratha

makes **4**
preparation time **10 minutes**
cooking time **10 minutes**

Meetha paratha is usually enjoyed by children.

Ingredients

Wheat flour ∘ 100g
Sugar/ jaggery ∘ 40g
Ghee ∘ 40g (oil can also be used)
Water ∘ to prepare dough

Method

- Prepare soft dough by adding water gradually in wheat flour and keep it for ½ hour.
- Divide dough in four equal parts. Roll out each ball into 3" diameter disc.
- Put 10g sugar or jaggery in each rolled ball and close it by pressing tight with fingers.
- Roll out each sugar filled ball into 6" diameter disc slowly so that the sugar/ jaggery does not burst out.
- Shallow fry on hot tawa by applying ghee on both sides. Sugar will start melting so fry it on slow flame till it turns golden.
- Serve hot with curd or plain.

Nutritive value

Protein g	Energy kcal	Calcium mg	Iron mg	Carotene µg	Thiamin B1 mg	Riboflavin B2 mg	Niacin B3 mg
12.1	860	48	4.9	29	0.49	0.17	4.3

ℋalwa
Steamed and lightly fried pudding

makes **4 small bowls**
preparation time **10 minutes**
cooking time **20 minutes**

Ingredients

Wheat flour ∘ 100g
Ghee ∘ 100g
Sugar ∘ 100g
Water ∘ 250g
Almonds (chopped) ∘ 10g

Method

- Heat ghee in pan, add wheat flour in ghee and fry on slow flame till it turns golden.
- Add water gradually to have thick consistency and stir well to avoid formation of lumps.
- Add sugar, stir well, cook for 2-3 minutes for absorption of syrup.
- Remove from fire and garnish with chopped dry fruits.
- Serve hot.

Variation

- Besan (Bengal gram daal flour) – about 20g – can be added to wheat flour. Other dry fruits and coconut powder can be used as garnishing.
- Suji halwa can be prepared in the same method. Mix of water and milk in 50:50 ratio should be added to the suji after frying it in ghee to a light golden brown hue.

Nutritive Value

Protein g	Energy kcal	Calcium mg	Iron mg	Carotene µg	Thiamin B1 mg	Riboflavin B2 mg	Niacin B3 mg
14.9	1704	71	5.4	629	0.49	0.17	4.7

Doodh dalia
Milk porridge

makes **4 bowls**
preparation time **5 minutes**
cooking time **15 minutes**

Ingredients
Broken wheat (dalia) ∘ 100g
Sugar ∘ 50g
Ghee ∘ 5g
Milk ∘ 300g
Water ∘ 200g

Method
- Heat ghee in pressure cooker, sauté dalia for 2-3 minutes, add water and cook.
- After one whistle of the pressure cooker, slow down the gas and cook for 5 to 6 minutes on low flame.
- Open cooker after it is cool, add milk, sugar and cook for 4 to 5 minutes and stir it to avoid lump formation and sticking. Quantity of milk may vary depending .on the desired consistency.
- Mix well till the mixture is of even consistency.
- Serve hot for breakfast.

Value addition and variation
- Barley /Bajra dalia is also used for making doodh dalia. Dalia can be garnished with finely chopped dry fruits, raisins, chopped dates and cardamom/ elayichi powder.

Nutritive value

Protein g	Energy kcal	Calcium mg	Iron mg	Carotene µg	Thiamin B1 mg	Riboflavin B2 mg	Niacin B3 mg
11.8	590	41	5.3	79	0.45	0.17	5.5

Maize

Maize is widely consumed in Mewar, the southern part of Rajasthan, both in the tender (bhutta) and the matured/ dry form. The dry maize grains are used in three different forms—as whole, dalia and flour. A variety of preparations are created from dry and tender maize. Maize, also known as corn in some countries, is popular in the western countries too, especially in the USA, which is the largest producer of maize in the world. It is also grown in China, Brazil and South America. Maize can only be produced in areas that do not have extreme cold temperature, as it is a cold-intolerant crop. Recipes of a few maize preparations follow.

Maize roti

makes **4 to 5 rotis**
preparation time **10 minutes**
cooking time **15 minutes**

Ingredients
Maize flour • 200g
Ghee • 20g
Salt • to taste
Luke warm water • for making dough

Method
• Add salt in the flour. Prepare smooth dough with warm water and knead well.
• Make balls. Make roti on rolling board by patting with palm, using a little water as and when required.
• Bake roti on tawa from both sides on medium flame and then bake on direct flame.
• Remove from fire and apply ghee on roti.

Combination
Maize roti is enjoyed with mixed daal, vegetable curry, kadhi, curd, butter milk and jaggery (gur).

Value addition and variation
• Add finely chopped green leafy vegetables in the dough.
• Bajra and jowar flour can be used to make roti.
• Paratha of the same leftover dough can be prepared.
• Baking of roti on earthen tawa gives a different taste to maize roti.

Nutritive Value

Protein g	Energy kcal	Calcium mg	Iron mg	Carotene μg	Thiamin B1 mg	Riboflavin B2 mg	Niacin B3 mg
22.2	864	20	4.6	300	0.8	0.2	3.6

Makki ka dhokla
Steamed fluffy savoury cones

makes **6 pieces**
preparation time **20 minutes**
cooking time **35 minutes**

Makki ka dhokla is a very popular dish of Mewar. It is generally prepared during winter. Hot dhoklas are served with ghee or oil and mixed daal. Dhoklas are also enjoyed with curd and sugar. Finely chopped vegetables and peas can be added to the flour for a healthy contemporary touch. This increases the nutritive value of dhoklas.

Ingredients

Maize flour (coarse) ∘ 250g
*Papad khar ∘ 5g
Whole green chillies ∘ 2-3
Garlic (optional) ∘ 2 cloves
Coriander leaves ∘ 4 stems
Ginger ∘ ½" piece
Red chilli powder ∘ 5g
Carom (ajwain) ∘ 5g
Cumin (jeera) ∘ 5g
Ground coriander
    ∘ 5g coarsely ground seeds
Salt ∘ to taste
Water ∘ for making dough

Method

- Finely chop green chillies, garlic, ginger and coriander leaves.
- Mix well salt, papad khar, dry ingredients and chopped green masala in the flour. To taste adequacy of salt and papad khar, add one drop of water in small portion of mixture and taste. If required add a little salt and papad khar accordingly. Prepare hard dough and knead it well.
- Divide dough in six equal parts. Shape dhoklas into cones and make a tiny hole at the pointed tip.
- Fill ⅓ of pressure cooker with water and keep iron or steel ring at the bottom. Keep a jali (perforated steel plate) on the ring. Boil the water.
- Arrange dhoklas on jali (perforated steel plate) in 3-4 rows. Close the lid. Do not put the pressure weight.
- Steam cook dhoklas for 20 minutes on high flame. Lower the flame and cook for another 10 minutes. Remove the lid.
- Put a knife in the dhokla, it should come out clean if done.
- Serve hot with mixed daal.

Note - Papad khar is an alkaline salt obtained from mines. It is an essential and vital ingredient in making papads and maize dhokla. It makes the papad crispy yet soft and helps it expand in size when fried. It is white in colour.

Nutritive Value

Protein g	Energy kcal	Calcium mg	Iron mg	Carotene µg	Thiamin (B1) mg	Riboflavin (B2) mg	Niacin (B3) mg
29.6	890	112	6.9	256	1.0	0.3	5.1

Raab
Savoury porridge

makes **4 bowls**
preparation time **5 minutes**
cooking time **45 minutes**

Ingredients
Maize dalia • 50g
Butter milk • 750 ml
Cumin (jeera) • 5g powder
Salt • to taste

Raab is a semi-solid preparation of cereals and buttermilk. Dalia (broken cereal) and flour is cooked in buttermilk. Cereals can be wheat, maize, bajra and barley. In rural areas, raab is cooked in earthen pots. In urban homes a pressure cooker or a pan is used to prepare raab. Wheat and barley raab is called maheri and is popular in eastern Rajasthan while maize raab is common in the southern regions of the state. Maheri is generally served with hot milk and sugar.

Raab is usually taken in the morning or at lunch time. In winter, hot raab is popular while in summer cold raab is preferred. It has now become a very popular starter at parties.

Method
Raab can be prepared in two ways

- Heat butter milk in pressure cooker, stirring it continuously to avoid curdling. Add dalia in butter milk and cook it without lid on high flame. Stir continuously till first boil. Cook on medium flame for 20 minutes. Stir from time to time. When the grain is soft, close the lid. Pressure cook for 20 minutes on slow flame. Add salt and roasted jeera powder.

or

- Cook maize dalia in water in pressure cooker till 20 minutes on slow flame. Add butter milk and stir well. Pressure cook it on slow flame for 20 minutes. Add salt and roasted jeera powder. Risk of curdling of buttermilk reduces in this method.

Value Addition and Variation
- Finely chopped leafy vegetables and grated carrot can be added to raab.
- Urad daal powder can be added to raab for thickening the consistency.
- Raab can also be prepared from maize flour.

Nutritive Value

Protein g	Energy kcal	Calcium mg	Iron mg	Carotene µg	Thiamin (B1) mg	Riboflavin (B2) mg	Niacin (B3) mg
12.4	301	81.5	2.4	71	0.5	0.1	1.0

$\mathcal{M}$aize papadi/ khichiya
Roasted and fried crispies

makes **25 pieces**
preparation time **10 minutes**
cooking time **40 minutes**

Ingredients

Maize flour • 250g
Papad khar (coarsely ground
   papad) • 5g
Cumin (jeera) • 5g
Carom (ajwain) • 5g
Oil • 20g
Salt and red chilli powder
   • to taste
Water • 500ml

Method

- Add masala and papad khar in flour and mix well.
- Put oil and water in pressure cooker and boil it. Add flour gradually in boiling water and keep stirring to avoid lumps.
- Cook on high flame till one whistle. Cook for 40 minutes on slow flame.

- Remove from fire, take out small portions of mixture, knead well with the help of a small steel bowl.
- Make small balls and roll out thin (like chapatis) using rolling pin and board or a chapati maker. Keep the ball between two layers of plastic sheet in the chapati maker and press it to get desired size of papadi.
- Spread papadi on plastic sheet and dry it in the sun. Turn the side once during the day. It will take roughly 2 to 3 days in the sun for proper drying. Store dried papadi in air-tight container.
- Papadi can be deep fried or roasted and is enjoyed in winter.

Variation
- Sev can be prepared with this dough using sev machine and is also sun dried. Sev is deep fried and served as a snack.
- Wheat flour can also be used to make papadi. Wheat flour and maize flour in proportion of 1:1 can also be taken to make papadi.

Nutritive value

Protein g	Energy kcal	Calcium mg	Iron mg	Carotene µg	Thiamin (B1) mg	Riboflavin (B2) mg	Niacin (B3) mg
29.5	1074	155	6.95	255	0.8	0.3	4.7

Tender maize or sweet corn (bhutta)

It is widely used in Mewar for making different
preparations. Hot bhutta pakodi in the rainy season
is a real treat. Jajaria is a mouth-watering sweet dish
and is prepared on special occasions. Scraped bhutta
grains are used for making sabzi, pulav and cutlets.
Bhutta cobs are relished as roasted, boiled and fried.
A few preparations are given here.

$\mathcal{B}$hutta pakodi
Fried savoury nuggets

makes **8 plates**
preparation time **20 minutes**
cooking time **15 minutes**

Ingredients

Tender maize (bhutta)
  ◦ 1 kg (300g grain)
Gram daal flour
  (Bengal gram/ besan) ◦ 250g
Whole green
  chillies ◦ 3-4
Ginger ◦ 1" piece
Green coriander ◦ 3-4 stems
Lemon juice ◦ 1 tea spoon
Fennel seeds (saunf) and
  garam masala ◦ 5g each
Red chilli powder ◦ 10g
Salt ◦ to taste
Oil ◦ for deep frying

Method

* Scrape grains from bhutta with the help of a knife. If grains are big, grind in mixer for a few seconds. Finely chop green chillies, ginger and coriander leaves.
* Mix all masala in besan (Bengal gram daal flour). Add water gradually to make batter. Batter should be of medium consistency.

- Put bhutta grains in batter and a few drops of lemon juice, mix well.
- Fry small balls in hot oil till these turn golden.
- Serve hot crisp pakodi with green chutney or tomato sauce.

Variation
- Like bhutta pakodi, green tender chana (called leelva in Mewar region) is also used for making pakodi.
- Mixed vegetable pakodi with bhutta grains and leelva can also be prepared.

Nutritive value

Protein g	Energy kcal	Calcium mg	Iron mg	Carotene µg	Thiamin (B1) mg	Riboflavin (B2) mg	Niacin (B3) mg	Vit.C mg
66.1	2205	167	16.5	418	4.5	1.0	6.2	20.5

$\mathcal{B}$hutta sabzi
Sweet corn curry

makes **6 bowls**
preparation time **20 minutes**
cooking time **20 minutes**

Ingredients

Bhutta/sweet corn ∘ 1kg
  (300g grains)
Oil ∘ 30g
Onion (medium size) ∘ 2
Garlic ∘ 5-6 cloves
Ginger ∘ 1" piece
Whole green chillies ∘ 3
  (finely chopped)
Curd (beaten) ∘ 50g

Turmeric ∘ 5g
Cumin ∘ 5g
Whole garam masala
  (black pepper, cloves,
  cinnamon) ∘ 5g
Coriander leaves ∘ 3-4 stems
Asafoetida (heeng) ∘ a pinch
Red chilli powder ∘ 10g
Salt ∘ to taste

Bhutta sabzi is a routine dish in a
Mewari kitchen during the rainy
season. It is relished by both young and
old in the family.

Method

- Scrap bhutta grains (sweet corn) with the help of a knife. Grind onion, ginger and garlic in the grinder.
- Heat oil in pressure cooker, add whole garam masala and sauté till it cracks; add onion paste and fry till it turns golden-brown.
- Add dry spices and lightly beaten curd. Stir well till it releases oil.
- Now add the sweet corn with chopped green chillies and mix well.
- Add one glass of water for making the gravy. Close the lid and cook for 10 minutes on medium flame till grains become tender.
- Remove from fire and garnish with chopped coriander leaves.
- Serve hot with chapati, puri or paratha.

Variation / Value addition

- Green tender chana sabzi is also cooked in a similar way.
- Finely chopped spinach can be added while preparing bhutta sabzi.
- Bhutta/sweet corn sabzi without gravy can also be prepared.

Nutritive Value

Protein g	Energy kcal	Calcium mg	Iron mg	Carotene µg	Thiamin (B1) mg	Riboflavin (B2) mg	Niacin (B3) mg	Vit.C mg
18.9	764	207	5.1	167	0.7	0.6	0.8	29.6

$\mathcal{B}$hutta pulav
Sweet corn pulao

makes **4 bowls**
preparation time **5 minutes**
cooking time **15 minutes**

Ingredients

Rice • 100g
Oil • 15g
Bhutta grains/
   Sweet corn • 100g
Ginger • ½" piece
Whole green chillies • 2

Whole garam masala • 5g
Coriander leaves • 3 stems
Salt • to taste
Red chilli powder and
   turmeric • optional
Water • 200ml

Method
- Wash rice and soak for ½ an hour. Cut ginger and green chillies in small pieces.
- Heat oil in a pan, add whole garam masala and let it crack.
- Add bhutta grains, chopped ginger and green chillies, sauté for 2-3 minutes.
- Add rice, stir well. Add water and salt. Now cover and cook.
- Remove when rice is fully cooked.
- Garnish with finely chopped coriander leaves and serve hot.

Combination
Serve hot with curd, chutney, achaar and salad.

Variation
- Green tender chana (leelva) can be added.

Nutritive Value

Protein g	Energy kcal	Calcium mg	Iron mg	Carotene µg	Thiamin (B1) mg	Riboflavin (B2) mg	Niacin (B3) mg	Vit.C mg
11.5	610	20.7	4.0	41	0.2	0.3	2.5	11

Jajaria
Party dessert

Jajaria is a delicious sweet dish prepared from young and tender, milky bhutta grains. It is a delicacy of south Rajasthan. It is served as a dessert in parties and festivals.

makes **6 bowls**
preparation time **25 minutes**
cooking time **40 minutes**

Ingredients

Tender bhutta ∘ 1kg (300g grains)
Ghee ∘ 200g
Milk ∘ 1kg
Sugar ∘ 100g
Dry fruits ∘ 20g (finely chopped)

Method

- Scrape out bhutta grains with the help of a knife and grind grains to a fine paste. Sieve paste in strainer to remove fibre.
- Heat ghee in a pan and fry bhutta paste till it turns golden and ghee is released.
- Add milk and boil till it thickens like kheer. Add sugar and boil again for 5 minutes.
- Garnish with chopped dry fruits and serve hot.
- Fried bhutta paste can be stored in the refrigerator for a day or two.

Variation

- Green tender chana can also replace bhutta grains while making jajaria. Method is the same.

Nutritive value

Protein g	Energy kcal	Calcium mg	Iron mg	Carotene µg	Thiamin (B1) mg	Riboflavin (B2) mg	Niacin (B3) mg	Vit.C mg
48.6	3374	1285	6.5	1826	1.2	2.5	2.2	18

Bhutta barfi
Sweet corn squares, a sweetmeat

makes **30 pieces**
preparation time **30 minutes**
cooking time **30 minutes**

Ingredients
Tender bhutta • 1kg (300g grains)
Sugar • 200g
Khoya • 300g
Ghee • 50g
Cardamom (elayichi) • 4-5
Water • 50 ml to make syrup

Method
- Scrape grains (sweet corn) from the cob of the bhutta with a knife.
- Grind grains in mixture to get paste, sieve it to remove the fibre, fry in ghee on slow flame till it turns golden and ghee is released. Now mix khoya in this paste and fry till it browns.
- Make syrup of 1½ thread consistency in a separate pan.
- Add the fried mixture and the cardamom powder to the syrup and mix well.

- Spread the mixture on a greased plate. Cut equal pieces when the mixture has cooled and partially solidified.
- Serve and enjoy the fresh barfi with friends and relatives.

Variation
- Green chana (leelva) can be used to make barfi in the same manner. It is called leelva barfi.

Nutritive Value

Protein g	Energy kcal	Calcium mg	Iron mg	Carotene μg	Thiamin (B1) mg	Riboflavin (B2) mg	Niacin (B3) mg	Vit.C mg
74.1	2860	2895	3.3	843	1.0	1.7	3.0	36

Bajra is a millet grown in western and central Rajasthan. It is consumed in the winter season. Comparatively it is very rich in minerals and vitamins as shown in Appendix Table 1. The common preparations are roti, kheech, kheechada and raab. Bajra gudmudia is prepared on special occasions. Bajra roti is relished with butter and jaggery in addition to daal and chutney.

Bajra kheech
Porridge / kedgeree

makes **4 bowls**
preparation time **60 minutes**
cooking time **45 minutes**

Method of debranning – Water is sprinkled over cereals and kept for 30-40 minutes to make the outer bran layer soft. Then the grain is hand pounded with the aid of a mortar and pestle (*hamamdasta*). If the grains are still dry, sprinkle more water, as the grains should be moist when pounding. After the first phase of pounding, the grains are sifted for removing the outer bran fibre. This process is repeated 3-4 times to remove the bran completely. Debranned cereals cook very soft and develop a delicious taste.

Ingredients
Debranned bajra ◦ 250g
Milk ◦ 100ml
Ghee ◦ 30g
Coconut powder ◦ 10g
Water ◦ 400ml

Kheech is a common cereal preparation enjoyed in the state. Bajra kheech is popular in western and central Rajasthan while maize and wheat kheech are common in the southern part. Kheech is prepared from debranned whole cereals—bajra, maize and wheat. Debranning cereals is a process of removing bran (outer layer) of cereals. Debranned wheat, bajra and maize are now available in the market as well.

Method
- Boil water in pressure cooker, put debranned bajra and boil for 2-3 minutes.
- Add milk and cook till grain becomes soft. Close pressure cooker and cook on slow flame for 30 minutes.
- Remove from flame when pressure is released, place the kheech in a serving bowl and garnish with coconut powder.
- Serve hot with ghee.

Variation
- Whole moth or moong in the proportion of 1:¼ can be added in bajra.

Note - Do not confuse bran – which is the soft outer layer of the grain and is part of the grain with nutritive value – from the coarse, hard covering or skin of the grain, which is chaff or husk. This is removed at mills in the initial stages through threshing and winnowing. Processed debranned wheat flour which is freely available in the market uses a method to retain some of the nutritive value of the bran fibre.

Nutritive value

Protein g	Energy kcal	Calcium mg	Iron mg	Carotene µg	Thiamin (B1) mg	Riboflavin (B2) mg	Niacin (B3) mg
32.7	1305	265	21.0	563	0.9	0.8	6.2

Bajra gudmudia
Fried cookies, a tea snack

makes **12 tikkies (cookies)**
preparation time **10 minutes**
cooking time **15 minutes**

Ingredients

Bajra flour • 100g
Jaggery • 100g
Til • 10g
Oil • for deep frying

Method

- Add til and 5g of oil in flour. Dissolve jaggery in water and mix in flour to make hard dough.
- Shape small tikkis. Heat oil and deep fry on slow flame till they turn brown on both sides.
- Serve hot with coriander (dhania) chutney.

Nutritive value

Protein g	Energy kcal	Calcium mg	Iron mg	Carotene µg	Thiamin (B1) mg	Riboflavin (B2) mg	Niacin (B3) mg
13.8	1250	265	11.6	138	0.4	0.3	2.7

Bajra khichada
Kedgeree

makes **4 bowls**
preparation time **10 minutes**
cooking time **30 minutes**

Ingredients
Bajra • 100g
Moong chhilka daal • 50g
Ghee • 15g
Water • 300ml

Method
* Lightly grind bajra and moong daal separately in the grinder for making dalia. Mix the two.
* Put this mixture in the pressure cooker. Add water, salt and cook on medium high flame till one whistle. Reduce flame and cook the dalia for a further 25 minutes.
* Add ghee and serve hot.

Note - Debranned bajra can also be used.

Combination: Khichada can be combined with ghee and sugar, leafy vegetables or curd.

Nutritive value

Protein g	Energy kcal	Calcium mg	Iron mg	Carotene µg	Thiamin (B1) mg	Riboflavin (B2) mg	Niacin (B3) mg
23.6	663	104	10.2	269	0.6	0.4	3.4

Pulses are the main source of proteins and minerals in a vegetarian diet (see Appendix Table 2). The main pulses grown and consumed in Rajasthan are moong, urad, chana, moth and arhar. In Rajasthani cuisine, pulses are used in abundance. Some popular dishes prepared from pulses are bhujia, papad, mangodi, pakodi, besan (Bengal gram daal flour) gatte, kadhi, cutlets etc. Sweets like chakki and laddu are made of besan. Some common dishes have been presented in this chapter.

Power of Pulses

Damdaar Daalen

Daal is trendy food now. The simple daal-chawal, daal-roti can be transformed into a complete and tasty meal by itself, with creative variations and mixing different daals.

Mixed daal

This preparation is more nutritious as it contains four pulses.

makes **4 bowls**
preparation time **10 minutes**
cooking time **30 minutes**

Ingredients

Urad daal without
   skin (chhilka) • 20g
Urad daal with chhilka • 10g
Moong chhilka daal • 10g
Chana daal • 10g
Ghee • 10g
Turmeric • 3g

Garam masala powder • 5g
Ginger • ½" piece
Garlic (optional) • 4 cloves
Whole cumin (jeera) • a pinch
Asafoetida (heeng) • a pinch
Red chilli powder • to taste
Salt • to taste

Method

- Wash all the daals and put in the pressure cooker. Add water, salt and turmeric. Cook on high flame till one whistle. Slow down the fire and cook for another 5 minutes.
- Grind ginger, garlic and chilli into a fine paste. Warm ghee in a small pan, add cumin and asafoetida, allow them to crackle in the ghee. Add the prepared paste and sauté it. Turn off the gas and add red chilli powder to the sautéed paste in the end to avoid the chilli powder getting burnt.
- Temper the boiled mixture of daals with this paste while it remains crackling hot and mix well.
- Garnish with coriander leaves and serve hot.

Nutritive value

Protein g	Energy kcal	Calcium mg	Iron mg	Carotene µg	Thiamin (B1) mg	Riboflavin (B2) mg	Niacin (B3) mg
11.7	270	67.4	4.5	109.7	0.2	0.2	1.1

*M*angodi / badi
Sundried lentil nuggets

Mangodis are small balls/ nuggets made of moong, urad or chawala daal paste which are sun-dried and preserved for 6 to 12 months. Mangodis are used for making sabzi (with or without gravy) and pulav.

Method
- Soak daal for 5-6 hours. Remove husk if chhilka daal (pulses with skin) is used.
- Grind daal into a fine paste of medium consistency.
- Add asafoetida, salt and beat it well until it becomes fluffy.
- Shape small balls out of the paste with fingers and place each of them on a plastic sheet – some distance apart – for drying in the sun. A plastic cone can be used for making the balls.
- Sundry for 4-5 days and store in air-tight container.

Variation
- For masala mangodi, add red chilli powder, coarse coriander powder, fennel and finely chopped coriander leaves to the paste.

Mangodi ki sabzi
Nuggets curry

makes **4 bowls**
preparation time **10 minutes**
cooking time **10 minutes**

Ingredients
Mangodi ∘ 50g
Ghee/ Oil ∘ 15g
Turmeric ∘ 3g
Coriander powder ∘ 3g
Cumin powder ∘ 3g
Onion ∘ 1 medium size
Ginger ∘ ½" piece
Green chilli ∘ 2
Red chilli powder ∘ 3g
Asafoetida (heeng) ∘ a pinch

Method
- Make a paste out of onions, green chillies and ginger.
- Heat oil in a pan, add cumin, asafoetida and add the paste; sauté till it turns golden brown.
- Break mangodi in small pieces and sauté in small quantity of oil/ghee.
- Add the fried mangodi and salt in the paste, mix well. Add water and cook for 10 minutes on medium flame.
- Temper it with red chilli powder. Garnish with chopped coriander leaves.

Note - Tempering is a process wherein spices are added one by one to hot oil, which is then added to the dish either in the beginning or in the end.

Variation
- Mangodi is prepared in combination with many vegetables and other food items like rice. Mangodi papad sabzi, potato mangodi, mangodi spinach, peas mangodi, mangodi mogri, mangodi rice pulav are some common, tasty but simple dishes.

Nutritive value

Protein g	Energy kcal	Calcium mg	Iron mg	Carotene µg	Thiamin (B1) mg	Riboflavin (B2) mg	Niacin (B3) mg	Vit.C mg
12.9	340	64.2	4.7	40.4	0.3	0.2	1.4	10.5

Kadhi pakodi
Batter-fried nuggets in tangy gravy

makes **4 bowls**
preparation time **15 minutes**
cooking time **30 minutes**

Ingredients

Bengal gram daal
  flour (besan) • 70g
Buttermilk • 400ml
Fenugreek seeds
  (methi dana) • 5g
Mustard (rai) • 5g

Cumin (jeera) • 5g
Red chilli powder • 5g
Turmeric • 5g
Ghee • 10g
Salt • to taste
Oil • for frying

Method

- Take 50g of Bengal gram daal flour (besan). Make a thin batter by adding water gradually. Beat it well.
- Heat oil in a pan, drop dollops of the batter in it with a spoon (or use your fingers) and fry medium size pakodis till they turn golden on all sides.
- Mix remaining 20g besan in buttermilk for preparing the kadhi (the curry). Add salt and turmeric powder and stir well.
- Keep pan on fire. Add 10g oil/ ghee in pan and heat it. Add fenugreek seeds, mustard seeds, cumin seeds and asafoetida (methi dana, rai, sabut jeera, heeng), green chopped chillies and washed sweet (meetha) neem leaves.

- After these start crackling and spluttering, add the Bengal gram daal flour (besan) and buttermilk mixture. Continuously stir till it begins to boil well. Turn down the flame and cook the kadhi for 15-20 minutes.
- Add the fried pakodis to the kadhi and cook for the next 5 minutes. Temper kadhi with cumin powder, asafoetida and red chilli powder.
- Garnish with chopped green coriander leaves and serve hot with rice, roti, bati and lapsi.

Variation and value addition
- Finely chopped fresh leafy geens like bathua saag, palak, kulfa, dried green chana leaves and radish can also be added to kadhi.

Nutritive value

Protein g	Energy kcal	Calcium mg	Iron mg	Carotene µg	Thiamin (B1) mg	Riboflavin (B2) mg	Niacin (B3) mg
17.8	545	159	4.1	90.3	0.3	0.1	1.7

Pakodi sabzi
Batter-fried nuggets in gravy

makes **4 bowls**
preparation time **10 minutes**
cooking time **20 minutes**

Ingredients

Bengal gram daal
   flour (besan) ∘ 100g
Curd ∘ 15g
Cloves ∘ 2
Red chilli powder ∘ 5g
Turmeric ∘ 3g
Coriander powder ∘ 5g

Oil for seasoning ∘ 5g
Coriander leaves ∘ 2 stems
Curry leaves ∘ 6-8 leaves
Asafoetida (heeng) ∘ a pinch
Salt ∘ to taste
Oil ∘ for deep frying pakodi
Water ∘ for gravy

Method

• Add salt in besan (Bengal gram daal flour). Prepare batter of pouring consistency by adding water gradually. Fry small size pakodi in hot oil.

• Heat oil/ ghee in pan. Add heeng, clove and jeera and allow it to crack. Add churned curd and stir well. Add salt and spices and sufficient quantity of water for gravy as pakodi will absorb water. Cook for 10 minutes. Add pakodi and cook for next 3 - 4 minutes.

• Garnish with chopped coriander leaves. Serve hot with roti, puri and paratha.

Variation

• Pakodi is used in making various preparations like curd raita, imli panna, keri panna and lemon panna.

Nutritive value

Protein g	Energy kcal	Calcium mg	Iron mg	Carotene µg	Thiamin (B1) mg	Riboflavin (B2) mg	Niacin (B3) mg
25.3	741	78	5.3	33.6	0.5	0.2	2.4

$\mathcal{B}$esan gatte
Gram flour rolls in gravy

makes **6 bowls**
preparation time **20 minute**
cooking time **20 minutes**

Ingredients

for the gatte:
Besan (Bengal gram daal flour)
  ∘ 200g
Oil for moyan ∘ 45g
Curd ∘ 30g
Coriander powder ∘ 5g
Red chilli powder ∘ 3g
Carom seeds (ajwain) ∘ 5g

Salt ∘ to taste
for the gravy:
Oil ∘ 20g
Whole garam masala
  ∘ 5g (clove, black pepper,
  cardamom and bay leaves)
Red chilli powder ∘ 5g
Asafoetida (heeng) ∘ a pinch
Turmeric ∘ 5g

Coriander (dhania)
  powder ∘ 5g
Ginger ∘ ½" piece
Garlic cloves ∘ 4-5
Onion ∘ 1 medium size
Curd ∘ 20g
Coriander leaves ∘ 4-5 stems
Salt ∘ to taste
Water ∘ for gravy

Method
- Add salt, ground masala, 10g of curd and oil for moyan in besan (Bengal gram daal flour) and mix well. Add water and knead well to prepare soft dough.
- Make small rolls of 1 inch thickness and 3-4 inches in length out of the dough. Put these rolls in boiling water and boil for 10-15 minutes till these start floating on water and the surface of the rolls appears grainy and their size increases. Strain them out of the water and cut into smaller pieces. Retain the hot and boiled water for adding to the gravy.
- For preparing the gravy, make a paste of onion, ginger and garlic. Heat oil in a pan, add asafoetida, cumin, whole garam masala and allow them to splutter.
- Add paste and sauté till it turns golden-brown. Now add beaten curd and stir well.
- Add water for gravy and boil. Put gatte in gravy and cook for 5 minutes.
- Garnish with chopped coriander leaves and serve hot with chapati, puri and paratha.

Variation
- Boiled gattas can be deep fried before adding to the gravy.
- Fried gattas can be added in pulav.
- Gatta sabzi without gravy can also be prepared.

Nutritive value

Protein g	Energy kcal	Calcium mg	Iron Mg	Carotene μg	Thiamin (B1) mg	Riboflavin (B2) mg	Niacin (B3) mg	Vit.C mg
42.8	1431	185	11.7	271	1.1	0.4	5.0	11

$\mathcal{S}$abut moth
Whole turkish gram beans/ dew beans

makes **4 bowls**
preparation time **10 minutes**
cooking time **10 minutes**

Ingredients
Moth • 50g
Chana • 10g
Salt • to taste
Turmeric • a pinch
Cumin (jeera) • 5g
Red chilli powder • 5g
Green chillies (chopped • 2
Asafoetida (heeng) • a pinch
Onion (small, chopped) • 1
Oil • 10g

Moth is grown in the semi-desert and desert regions of Marwar where water is a scarce commodity and there is almost no access to vegetables and greens. Simple home preparations from whole moth, variations of savouries like bhujia, namkeen, papad and the wholesome kadhi are common dishes during mealtimes here.

Method

- Soak moth and chana in the morning for 6 hours. Drain the water and wait overnight for germination.
- Boil the soaked moth in pressure cooker till one whistle on high flame. Remove it from fire and open the lid of the pressure cooker.
- Heat oil in a pan. Add asafoetida (heeng), cumin (jeera) and other dry masala. Saute chopped onion and green chillies; add boiled moth and chana to it. Mix well on low-medium flame.
- Garnish with coriander leaves and serve hot.

Nutritive value

Protein g	Energy kcal	Calcium mg	Iron mg	Carotene µg	Thiamin (B1) mg	Riboflavin (B2) mg	Niacin (B3) mg	Vit.C mg
14.1	344	152	5.6	95	0.15	0.1	1.6	-

Besan chakki
Bengal gram daal flour candy

makes **15 pieces**
preparation time **10 minutes**
cooking time **45 minutes**

Ingredients

Bengal gram daal
  flour (besan) ∘ 200g
Sugar ∘ 160g
Ghee ∘ 180g
Water ∘ 200ml
Chopped dry fruits
  ∘ to garnish (optional)

Method

- Add 30g of ghee in besan and rub nicely to mix well. Add water gradually to make hard dough.
- Make muthia (fist shaped balls) and deep fry till golden in colour.
- Grind it to get a coarse powder. Heat remaining ghee, add the coarse fried mixture and fry on slow flame till it turns dark brown and starts giving out a pleasing fragrance.

- Make sugar syrup of 1½ thread consistency by adding sugar in boiling water on medium flame and stirring till it thickens. Add fried mixture in syrup and stir continuously till it mixes well.
- Spread it on a greased plate (thali) and level the top with a spatula.
- Garnish liberally with chopped dry fruits (optional) when the syrupy mixture is still warm and partially soft.
- When it cools down, cut into square pieces and serve.

Variation
- Instead of water, milk can be used for making dough for muthias.
- Khoya/ mawa can be used in the proportion of 1:¼

Nutritive value

Protein g	Energy kcal	Calcium mg	Iron mg	Carotene µg	Thiamin (B1) mg	Riboflavin (B2) mg	Niacin (B3) mg
41.6	3000	131	10.8	1338	1.0	0.4	4.8

Vegetables in a Variety

Sabziyan Swaad-bhari

Use of vegetables in daily diet is low in the western and southern parts of Rajasthan because of low production due to a combination of arid semi-desert and desert as well as hilly terrains. In these areas, it is common practice to include different preparations of besan (Bengal gram daal flour), bhutta (maize) and dry vegetables like ker sangria as sabzi (vegetables dish) in the menu. Improved roads and transport facilities have eased out the situation and made vegetables and fruits available in cities and towns of this region. Villagers sundry or pickle seasonal winter vegetables and use them in summer.

Ratalu sabzi
Yam curry

makes **4 servings**
Preparation time **20 minutes**
Cooking time **20 minutes**

Ratalu – yam or sweet potato – is a purple-
pigmented root vegetable grown in the
southern part of Rajasthan. It is long in
shape and the flesh inside is purple in
colour. It is available mainly in winter and
can be stored for 2-3 months.

Ingredients

Ratalu ∘ 100g
Onion (medium) ∘ 1
Ginger ∘ ½" piece
Garlic (optional) ∘ 4-5 cloves
Oil ∘ 30g
Curd ∘ 30g
Red chilli powder ∘ 5g

Turmeric ∘ 3g
Cumin powder ∘ 5g
Coriander powder ∘ 5g
Green chillies ∘ 2
Asafoetida (heeng) ∘ a pinch
Coriander leaves ∘ 3-4 stems
Salt ∘ to taste

Method

- Apply a little oil in hands and scrape off the outer skin of ratalu. Cut into medium size pieces and deep fry them.
- Make a paste of onion, ginger, garlic and green chillies.
- Heat oil in a pan and add asafoetida, cumin and the paste. Saute till it turns golden.
- Add beaten curd, all the dry masala and fry for 5 minutes on a slow flame. Put fried ratalu pieces in the masala. Add water and pressure cook till one whistle.
- Garnish with finely chopped coriander leaves and serve hot with chapati, puri or paratha.

Variation

- Ratalu can be cooked without gravy as a semi-dry sabzi. Ratalu slices can be fried and used as a snack by sprinkling salt and black pepper powder. Ratalu pakodi is also a common snack. Ratalu pulav is a delicacy in which fried ratalu pieces are added to the pulav.

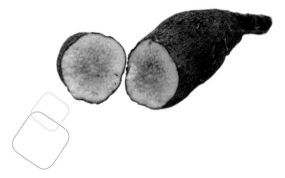

Nutritive value

Protein g	Energy kcal	Calcium mg	Iron mg	Carotene µg	Niacin B3	Vit. C mg
2.0	406	60	1.7	87	0.3	16

Bharwa besan mirch
Stuffed chillies

makes **6**
preparation time **10 minutes**
cooking time **10 minutes**

Ingredients

Large green
  chillies (mirch) ∘ 100g
Besan (Bengal gram daal flour)
  ∘ 50g
Turmeric ∘ 3g

Dried mango powder
  (amchur)/ lemon juice ∘ 5g
Red chilli powder ∘ 3g
Garam masala ∘ 5g powder
Salt ∘ to taste
Oil ∘ 25g

This dish is to be prepared with special large size mirch (chilli), thick and yellowish in colour. It is grown during the rainy season in the southern and western parts of the state. This is used for making sabzi and bada.

Method

- Wash chillies in fresh water. Slit vertically from one side and remove seeds.
- Roast besan on slow fire. Remove from fire, add salt, amchur/ lemon juice, garam masala powder and half the quantity of oil. Sprinkle water and mix well. Stuff some amount of the besan mixture into each of the chillies and press with fingers so that the besan does not spill out.
- Heat oil in a pan and add asafoetida and cumin. Put the stuffed mirch in it. Sprinkle water and cover with a lid. Cook for 8-10 minutes on a slow flame.
- Serve hot for lunch or dinner.

Variation

- Instead of besan, mashed potato mixed with the same spices can be stuffed into mirch and served.

Nutritive value

Protein g	Energy kcal	Calcium mg	Iron mg	Carotene µg	Thiamin (B1) mg	Riboflavin (B2) mg	Niacin (B3) mg	Vit.C mg
13.3	440	58	7.1	243	0.4	1.3	2.3	111

Mirchi bada
Fried chilli fingers

makes **6 pieces**
preparation time **10 minutes**
cooking time **15 minutes**

It is a popular snack in Rajasthan. Mirchi bada of Jodhpur is famous.

Ingredients

Mirch (thick, with a yellow tinge in the skin) ∘ 100g
Besan ∘ 100g
Potato ∘ 3 medium size
Amchur (dried green mango powder) ∘ 5g

Garam masala powder ∘ 5g
Turmeric ∘ a pinch
Salt ∘ to taste
Cooking soda ∘ a pinch
Coriander leaves ∘ 2-3 stems
Oil ∘ for deep frying

Method

- Boil potato and mash it. Add salt, other ingredients and finely chopped coriander leaves.
- Slit vertically mirch from one side and remove seeds. Stuff with potato masala.
- Add salt and a pinch of soda in besan (Bengal gram daal flour). Prepare batter of medium consistency by adding water. Dip stuffed mirch in batter for coating.
- Heat oil and fry coated mirch on medium flame till it turns golden.
- Serve hot with green coriander chutney/ sauce/ tamarind (imli) chutney.

Nutritive value

Protein g	Energy kcal	Calcium mg	Iron mg	Carotene µg	Thiamin (B1) mg	Riboflavin (B2) mg	Niacin (B3) mg	Vit.C mg
22.4	816	247	9.7	225	0.6	0.5	5.6	28.5

Kachha kela chhilka sabzi
Green banana peel curry

Peels scraped out of fresh vegetables like green banana (kachha kela), bottle gourd (lauki), ribbed/ snake gourd (tauri) and green peas make vegetable chhilka (peels) sabzi.

makes **4 bowls**
preparation time **10 minutes**
cooking time **10 minutes**

Ingredients

Kachha kela
    (Green banana) ∘ 100g
Oil ∘ 10g
Besan (Bengal gram
    daal flour) ∘ 10g
Green chillies ∘ 1
Red chilli powder ∘ 5g
Coriander powder ∘ 5g
Turmeric ∘ 3g
Amchur
    (dry mango powder) ∘ 3g
Carom seeds (ajwain) ∘ 3g
Asafoetida (heeng) ∘ a pinch

Method

• Peel the green banana retaining a little portion of the pulp. Cut peels in small round pieces and soak in water to avoid blackening.
• Heat oil in a pan, add asafoetida (heeng), carom seeds (ajwain) and allow them to crack and splutter.
• Add pieces of the peel (chhilka) and all the dry masala.
• Sprinkle a little water for cooking. Cover with lid and cook for 5-7 minutes on slow fire till peels soften.
• Take off the lid and sprinkle besan and water in it. Cover and cook again for 2 minutes. Finally add dry mango powder (amchur).
• Serve hot with roti, paratha or puri.

Variation
• A vegetable dish of fresh bottle gourd (lauki), ribbed/ snake gourd (tauri) peels is also prepared in a similar way.

Note - The nutritive value of peels is not available.

Dried vegetables curry

makes **3 bowls**
preparation time **5 minutes**
cooking time **5 minutes**

Ingredients

Dried vegetables ∘ 50g
Oil ∘ 15g
Cumin (jeera) ∘ 3g
Red chili powder ∘ 3g
Turmeric ∘ 3g
Coriander (dhania)
   powder ∘ 3g
Dried mango powder
   (amchur) ∘ 5g
Garam masala powder ∘ 5g
Onion ∘ 1 medium size
Ginger piece ∘ ½" piece
Green chillies ∘ 1-2
Coriander leaves ∘ 3-4 stems
Asafoetida (heeng) ∘ a pinch
Salt ∘ to taste

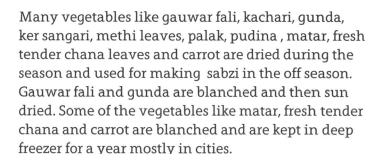

Many vegetables like gauwar fali, kachari, gunda, ker sangari, methi leaves, palak, pudina , matar, fresh tender chana leaves and carrot are dried during the season and used for making sabzi in the off season. Gauwar fali and gunda are blanched and then sun dried. Some of the vegetables like matar, fresh tender chana and carrot are blanched and are kept in deep freezer for a year mostly in cities.

For blanching, tie the vegetable pieces / peas in clean thin cloth (potli). Boil water in a pan, add salt in water in proportion of ½ tea spoon per kg of vegetables. Put the potli in boiling water for 2 minutes. Take out potli from water and immediately dip into cold water. This will stop further cooking and will also destroy bacteria due to sudden change in temperature. The vegetables are then sun-dried for 3-4 days or are kept in deep freezer after packing in polythene bags. Dried vegetables are stored in air-tight containers.

Method

- Soak dried vegetable in small quantity of water for 1 to 2 hours depending upon the type of vegetable, for example, leafy vegetables are soaked only for 10 to 15 minutes. Do not drain water.
- Make paste of green chilli and onion.
- Heat oil in a pan. Add jeera, heeng and paste, sauté till golden brown.
- Add soaked vegetable and dry masala and cook for 5 to 10 minutes till tender. Add amchur and garam masala powder. Garnish with coriander leaves.
- Serve hot with roti, puri and paratha.

Variation

- Dried gaur fali can be deep fried. Salt and red chilli powder are sprinkled and the fries are served as snack.

Pach kuta / ker sangri
The mix of five

makes **4 bowls**
preparation time **10 minutes**
cooking time **30 minutes**

Pach Kuta is a speciality of western Rajasthan. It is typical desert food where the local harvest – beans, berries, seeds and fruits – are tempered with spices. Pach Kuta is a mix of five plant products—ker, sangari/ sangri, kumatia, kachari and gunda. This is also known as ker sangari and is easily available in the market.

Ingredients

Ker sangri • 100g
Oil • 30g
Cumin (jeera) • 5g
Coriander (dhania)
  powder • 5g
Red chilli powder • 5g
Whole red chillies • 3
Fennel (saunf) • 2g
Dried mango (amchur)
  powder • 5g
Salt • to taste

Method

- Wash and soak ker sangri in water for 3 to 4 hours. Drain water and pressure cook till one whistle.
- Mix all the spices and salt in the boiled ker sangari. .
- Heat oil in a separate pan. Add asafoetida (heeng), cumin (jeera) and whole (sabut) red chillies. Add ker sangri and cook for 5 minutes.
- Add amchur (dried green mango powder) and mix well. It can be preserved for 3-4 days.
- Serve hot with chapatti, puri and paratha.

Variation

- Instead of amchur, mango achaar masala or tamarind (imli) pulp can be added.

Note: Nutritive value not available.

Meethi dana methi sabzi
Sweet-flavoured fenugreek seeds curry

makes **4 bowls**
preparation time **5 minutes**
cooking time **20 minutes**

Ingredients

Dana methi • 50g
Sugar • 20g
Raisins • 50g
Turmeric • 3g
Coriander powder • 5g

Amchur powder • 3g
Red chilli powder • 3g
Cumin (jeera) • 3g
Asafoetida (heeng) • a pinch
Oil • 15g
Salt • to taste

Method

- Soak fenugreek seeds/ dana methi in water overnight. Drain water. Add fresh water and pressure cook till one whistle. Open cooker and drain water.
- Wash the boiled seeds well in fresh running water 2 to 3 times, taking care to see that the outer skin remains unbroken, to avoid bitter taste in the prepared dish.
- Heat oil in pan. Add asafoetida (heeng), cumin (jeera) and the rest of the spices except the sour – mango powder (amchur) – and the sweet ingredients. Add a little water.
- Add sugar. Cook till the sugar is dissolved. Put dana methi and raisins in the pan. Cook for 5 minutes on slow flame. Add amchur (dry green mango powder).
- Serve hot.

Variation

- Dried tamarind (imli) pieces can be added instead of amchur. Soaked and chopped dates can be added.

Nutritive value

Protein g	Energy kcal	Calcium mg	Iron mg	Carotene µg	Thiamin (B1) mg	Riboflavin (B2) mg	Niacin (B3) mg
14.0	535	123.5	7.2	49.2	0.2	0.3	0.9

Dana methi papad
Curry of dried fenugreek seeds with papad

makes **4 bowls**
preparation time **5 minutes**
cooking time **20 minutes**

Ingredients

Dana methi • 50g
Papad (medium size) • 2
Oil • 25g
Red chilli powder • 5g
Turmeric • 3g
Cumin (jeera) • 2g
Amchur
(dry mango powder) • 3g
Garam masala
powder • a pinch
Salt • to taste

Dana methi sabzi as part of a
Rajasthani thali is a delicacy. Dana
methi (dried fenugreek seeds) is rich
in calcium and iron and is considered
good for joint pains and easy
digestion.(Appendix Table 6).

Method

- Soak dana methi in water overnight. Drain water. Add fresh water and pressure cook till one whistle. Open cooker and drain water.
- Wash the boiled dana methi in fresh running water at least 2 to 3 times without rubbing by hand and just allowing the water to run slowly over it. Rubbing may break outer bran and make the prepared dish bitter in taste.
- Heat oil in a pan and add asafoetida (heeng), cumin (jeera) and allow them to crack and splutter for 2-3 seconds. Add soaked dana methi and small pieces of roasted papad. Cook on slow flame for 4-5 minutes. Add amchur (dry green mango powder) and garam masala powder. Serve hot with chapatti, puri and paratha.

Variation

- Dana methi cooked with potato is another popular combination and a delicacy.

Nutritive value

Protein g	Energy kcal	Calcium mg	Iron mg	Carotene µg	Thiamin (B1) mg	Riboflavin (B2) mg	Niacin (B3) mg
20.3	496	80	3.3	62.7	0.4	0.3	1.5

Lahsan chutney
Garlic chutney

It is a very popular dish in Rajasthan especially in rural areas. The combination is with bati, kadhi, chawal. Lahsan adds aroma and taste to food, and has medicinal value.

makes **1 bowl**
preparation time **15 minutes**
cooking time **5 minutes**

Ingredients
Garlic bulb • 1 big blub
Whole (sabut) red chillies • 5
Turmeric • 3g
Coriander powder • 3g
Garam masala powder • 3g
Oil • 10g
Salt • to taste

Method
- Take out garlic cloves and peel them. Grind with red chillies and make a paste.
- Heat oil, add paste and masala.
- Cook till golden and oil is released from the paste.
- Serve hot at lunch or dinner.

Variation

- Chutney can be prepared without cooking by adding the powdered spices to the chilli-garlic paste. Coriander leaves can be added to it.

Nutritive value

Protein g	Energy kcal	Calcium mg	Iron mg	Carotene μg	Thiamin (B1) mg	Riboflavin (B2) mg	Niacin (B3) mg
4.8	186	31	0.83	54	0.5	0.2	1.3

$\mathcal{P}$apad sabzi
Papad curry

makes **4 bowls**
preparation time **5 minutes**
cooking time **5 minutes**

Ingredients

Moong daal papad ∘ 5 pieces
Oil ∘ 15g
Cumin (jeera) ∘ 3g
Turmeric ∘ 3g
Red chilli powder ∘ 5g
Curd ∘ 10g
Asafoetida (heeng) ∘ a pinch
Coriander leaves ∘ 2-3 stems
Salt ∘ to taste

Method

*   Roast papad and break in small pieces. Heat oil in pan, add heeng, jeera and allow to crack. Mix curd and other masala, stir well. Add water (for gravy) and bring to a boil. Add papad pieces and cook for 2-3 minutes.
*   Garnish with chopped coriander leaves. This is a quick-to-make recipe.

Nutritive value

Protein g	Energy kcal	Calcium mg	Iron mg	Carotene µg	Thiamin (B1) mg	Riboflavin (B2) mg	Niacin (B3) mg
24.8	489	90	3.9	52	0.5	0.2	2.4

Kacchi haldi ki sabzi
Raw turmeric dry curry

makes **2 bowls**
preparation time **15 minutes**
cooking time **10 minutes**

Ingredients

Kacchi haldi
   (render turmeric) ∘ 200g
Oil ∘ 50g
Fennel (saunf) ∘ 30g
(Mustard) rai ∘ 10g
Red chilli powder ∘ 10g
Black pepper ∘ 4-5 pcs
Cumin (jeera) ∘ 5
Dry mango
   (amchur) powder ∘ 5g
Salt ∘ to taste

Method

- Wash and peel the turmeric. Cut into small pieces.
- Dry grind saunf (fennel), dana methi (dried fenugreek seeds), rai (mustard seeds) and black pepper into coarse powder.
- Heat oil in pan, add jeera (cumin), heeng (asafoetida) and the coarsely ground spices. Then add the turmeric pieces. Mix it well. Cook for 5-7 minutes.
- Add salt, amchur (dry mango powder), chilli powder and cook for 4-5 minutes on a slow flame.
- Store the powdered mixture in a dry and air-tight container and keep the container in the fridge, so that you can enjoy the pickled curry over a few days.

Turmeric or haldi has several medicinal values and therefore it is advisable to consume this sabzi as a side dish. It can be stored for many days if kept in the refrigerator.

$\mathcal{M}$irchi ke tapore
Chilli dry dip

It is a common dish in rural areas and its popularity is now rising in urban areas too. It is quick to prepare and is used as a side dish.

makes **6 servings**
preparation time **5 minutes**
cooking time **8 minutes**

Ingredients
Thick green
    chillies (mirch) • 50g
Mustard (rai) • 3g
Oil • 5g
Turmeric • a pinch
Fennel and dry mango
    powder (saunf and amchur)
    • 10g each
Salt • to taste

Method
* Wash the chillies. Cut them in small round pieces and keep them soaked in water. This will help in removing the tiny seeds.
* Heat oil in pan. Add mustard, let it splutter and then add the chillies. Add salt, turmeric powder and fennel. Sauté for 3 to 4 minutes. Add amchur powder.
* Serve with meals and snacks

Nutritive value

Protein g	Energy kcal	Calcium mg	Iron mg	Carotene µg	Vit. C mg	Riboflavin (B2) mg	Niacin (B3) mg
1.5	59.5	15	2.2	88	55.5	0.2	0.45

Meat, Poultry and Fish

Maansahaari Zaika

A large population in Rajasthan is vegetarian but some of the groups – especially in tribal and rural areas – do enjoy non vegetarian food as well. They consume meat, chicken, eggs and fish—a good source of protein, minerals and calories (Appendix Table 5). These items are comparatively more expensive; people in Rajasthan consume non-vegetarian food on special occasions, particularly on festivals or at parties or during celebrations.

Laal maans
Rajasthani red meat curry

makes **12 servings**
preparation time **30 minutes**
cooking time **60 minutes**

Ingredients
Mutton pieces • 1kg
Mustard oil (preferably)
   • 100g
Onion (medium size) • 8
Garlic • 1 big bulb
Ginger • 2" piece
Whole garam masala • 6–8
   pieces each (clove, black
   pepper, cardamom and bay
   leaves)
Cumin • 10g
Red chilli powder • 10g
Coriander powder • 15g
Turmeric powder • 10g
Garam masala powder • 10g
Curd • 100g
Tomato • 5-6 medium size
Coriander leaves • 8 stems
Salt • to taste
Water • for gravy

Method
- Keep mutton pieces soaked in water for 10-15 minutes, wash 3-4 times in running water, shake off all the water and pat dry with a clean piece of cloth. Remove extra fat with a sharp edged knife.
- Cut half of the onions in long slices, and grind rest into paste. Make a paste of ginger and garlic separately.
- Heat oil in a pressure cooker, add whole garam masala, onion slices and sauté.
- Add the meat pieces, onion paste and fry for 15-20 minutes till it changes colour to golden and then to a deeper brown. Add beaten curd and chopped tomato, cook for 10 to 15 minutes till all ingredients mix well.
- Add ginger and garlic paste in the end and stir well. This retains the aroma of garlic and ginger. Fry all the ingredients well till oil is released.

- Add 400 ml water, salt and close the cooker. Pressure cook till one whistle and then cook for 15 minutes on slow flame.
- Garnish with finely chopped coriander leaves and serve hot with rice, roti or paratha after adjusting the liquid in the gravy as per requirement.

Variation

- In Rajasthan, dhundharu maans is also very famous. Dhundharu means adding fumes to the preparation which gives special aroma and flavour. For this process, keep a small steel bowl (katori) on the top of the cooked mutton. Keep a live coal in katori and pour 4-5g ghee on it. Cover the pan with lid. The fumes coming out from the ghee will be absorbed by meat.

Nutritive value

Protein g	Energy kcal	Calcium mg	Iron mg	Carotene µg	Thiamin (B1) mg	Riboflavin (B2) mg	Niacin (B3) mg	Vit. C mg
191.6	5681	1865	30.8	1070	0.77	1.8	3.22	122.5

Keema matar
Mince curry with peas

makes **6 servings**
preparation time **20 minutes**
cooking time **50 minutes**

Ingredients

Minced meat • 1kg
Oil • 90g
Onion (medium size) • 4
Ginger • 2" pcs
Green chillies • 3
Garlic • 1 big bulb
Peas • 300g
Tomatoes • 3-4 medium size

Coriander powder • 15g
Turmeric powder • 5g
Whole garam masala
• 5-6 pieces each (cloves, black pepper, bay leaves, cardamom)
Whole red chillies • 4 pcs
Red chilli powder • 10g
Salt • to taste

Method

• Buy minced meat, wash well in running water using a large strainer or colander and keep it soaked in water for 15 minutes. Peal and wash peas! Grind onion, ginger, garlic into fine paste.
• Heat oil in a pressure cooker, add whole garam masala, allow the whole spices to splutter and the cardamoms to crack. Now add onion-ginger-garlic paste and stir to mix.
• Fry all the ingredients well. Add keema and all the dry spices, stir well. Fry till oil is released and the keema is dark golden-brown.
• Add ½ a glass of water and cook in the pressure cooker with the lid on for 15 minutes on slow flame. When cool, open the cooker and add the green peas. Cook again for 7-8 minutes on slow flame in the pressure cooker.
• Garnish with finely chopped coriander leaves. Serve hot with paratha and puri.

Nutritive value

Protein g	Energy kcal	Calcium mg	Iron mg	Carotene µg	Thiamin (B1) mg	Riboflavin (B2) mg	Niacin (B3) mg	Vit.C mg
242	2468	325	7.3	291.5	0.8	-	3.35	60

Chicken curry

makes **10 servings**
preparation time **15 minutes**
cooking time **30 minutes**

Ingredients

Chicken • 1kg
Oil • 90g
Onion (medium size) • 6
Garlic • 1 big bulb
Ginger • 4" piece
Tomato • 4 medium size
Coriander powder • 15g
Turmeric powder • 5g
Cumin powder • 5g
Whole garam masala
   • 6-8 pieces each (cloves,
   black pepper, bay leaves,
   cardamom)
Salt • to taste

Method

- Wash chicken pieces in fresh running water. Grind onion, ginger and garlic into a fine paste.
- Heat oil in the pressure cooker, add whole garam masala and cumin (sabut jeera) and allow the spices to splutter.
- Add ginger-garlic-onion paste and stir well. Add chopped tomato pieces and cook till tomatoes are finely mixed with the paste.
- Add chicken pieces, mix well in the masala and fry till lightly golden in colour. Add one glass of water, salt and pressure cook for 15 minutes on slow flame. Adjust the gravy as required by adding more water or reducing the liquid by boiling the gravy on high flame.
- Garnish with finely chopped coriander leaves and serve hot with chapati and rice.

Nutritive value

Protein g	Energy kcal	Calcium mg	Iron mg	Carotene µg	Thiamin (B1) mg	Riboflavin (B2) mg	Niacin (B3) mg	Vit.C mg
269	2249	616	5.6	949	0.72	1.63	3.12	122.5

Egg curry

makes **4 servings**
preparation time **10 minutes**
cooking time **15 minutes**

Ingredients

Egg (Hen) ∘ 4
Oil ∘ 20g
Onion (medium size) ∘ 2
Ginger ∘ 1" piece
Garlic ∘ 6 cloves
Tomato (medium size) ∘ 1
Coriander powder ∘ 10g
Turmeric powder ∘ 3g

Whole garam masala
  ∘ 6-8 pieces each (cloves,
  black pepper, bay leaves,
  cardamom)
Red chilli powder ∘ 3g
Garam masala powder ∘ 5g
Salt ∘ to taste
Coriander leaves ∘ 3–4 stems

Method

- Boil eggs hard, allow them to cool by dipping the eggs in cold water and peel off the shells. The simplest way to peel the shell of a hard-boiled egg is to lightly crack the shell all over with the back of a spoon and then peeling off, using the end of the spoon's handle to scrape.
- Make a fine paste of onion, ginger, and garlic. Grind tomato separately to make puree.
- Heat oil in a pan, add whole garam masala and allow it to splutter, with the cardamoms cracking open. Add the paste and fry it till the paste turns golden in colour. Add tomato puree and cook it for 5 minutes. Add the dry spices, stir-fry lightly.
- Add water to make gravy, add salt, stir well, cook gravy and make it boil once.
- Add the boiled eggs in the gravy. Cook for another 5 minutes.
- Garnish with finely chopped coriander leaves and serve hot with chapati or rice.

Variation and value addition

- Peas and potatoes can be added to the egg curry. To add potatoes, boil 4 medium sized potatoes after cleaning the outer skin well in running water and slicing the potatoes half along the width. Peel off the outer skin after allowing the boiled potatoes to cool. Lightly brown the pieces and keep aside. These can be added to the gravy at a later stage, just before adding the eggs, allowing them to boil (covered) in the gravy for 2-3 minutes so that the flavours infuse well.
- The boiled eggs can be lightly fried and browned all over after peeling the shell and kept aside, to be added to the gravy later.

Nutritive value

Protein g	Energy kcal	Calcium mg	Iron mg	Carotene µg	Thiamin (B1) mg	Riboflavin (B2) mg	Niacin (B3) mg	Vit.C mg
22.6	517	171	5.8	1010	0.3	0.7	0.7	36

Fish curry

makes **6 bowls**
preparation time **45 minutes**
cooking time **20 minutes**

Fish is considered to be one of the best non-vegetarian foods as it contains good quality and easily digestive protein. It also has high calcium content.

Ingredients

Fish (Rohu/ katla) ∘ 1kg
Onion ∘ 5 medium size
Garlic ∘ 2 big bulb
Ginger ∘ 2" piece
Lemon ∘ 2 pcs
Tomato ∘ 3 medium size
Coriander leaves ∘ 4 stems
Coriander
   (dhania powder) ∘ 20g
Red chilli powder ∘ 10g
Fenugreek seeds
   (methi dana) ∘ 5g
Mustard (rai) ∘ 5g
Salt ∘ to taste
Water ∘ 400ml

Method

- Wash fish pieces thoroughly in running water and pat dry with a clean piece of cloth. Apply turmeric, salt and lemon juice on each piece. Keep these pieces marinated for 30 minutes. Wash these pieces again with running water.
- Grind onion, ginger, garlic, rai (mustard) and tomato separately.
- Heat oil in pan, add dana methi (fenugreek seeds), the spice paste and sauté the mixture. Now add tomato puree and cook for 5 minutes. Add salt and other spices and stir well.
- Add water and boil on slow flame for 5 minutes. Add fish pieces in masala and cover with lid. Cook for 15- 20 minutes.
- Remove from gas stove. Garnish with chopped coriander leaves.
- Serve hot with rice and chapati.

Nutritive value

Protein g	Energy kcal	Calcium mg	Iron mg	Carotene µg	Thiamin (B1) mg	Riboflavin (B2) mg	Niacin (B3) mg	Vit.C mg
178	1782	684	15.6	75.5	0.7	0.74	8.8	264.7

Fish fry (snack / starter)

makes **6 plates**
preparation time **45 minutes**
cooking time **20 minutes**

Ingredients

Fish (Rohu/ Katla/ Bachha) • 1kg
Besan (Bengal gram daal flour) • 50g
Semolina (suji) • 50g
Curd • 20g
Lemon • 1 for the juice
Garlic • 1 big bulb
Ginger • 3" piece
Turmeric powder • 20g
Red chilli powder • 10g
Garam masala powder • 15g
Chat masala • 10g
Salt • to taste

Method

- Take fish, preferably rohu. Clean by washing well in running water and pat dry with a clean piece of cloth. Apply turmeric and lemon juice and rub in a pinch of salt on each piece and keep the fish in a cool place for 20 minutes.
- Grind ginger and garlic to make a fine paste. Mix besan (Bengal gram daal flour), curd and dry spices in the paste. Marinate the fish with the prepared mixture and keep for ½ an hour.
- For frying the fish, take suji (semolina) in a plate and coat each piece with it.
- Heat mustard oil and deep fry the semolina-coated fish pieces on slow flame till they are golden brown. Prick to see if the fish is well-done inside. Raise the flame and brown it.
- Sprinkle chat masala, garam masala powder and salt; serve hot immediately with chutney.

Nutritive value

Protein g	Energy kcal	Calcium mg	Iron mg	Carotene µg	Thiamin (B1) mg	Riboflavin (B2) mg	Niacin (B3) mg	Vit.C mg
182	2278	657	13.5	135	0.8	0.8	9.0	231.7

India is known for festivals. A number of festivals are celebrated in different regions of Rajasthan which breaks the monotony of life. Special food is prepared on festivals which adds variety in the daily food routine. There are various traditional dishes made on different festivals. A few select preparations are given below.

The year begins with Makar Sakranti festival which is a solar event. The date of this festival remains constant over a long period—14 January. It is also a harvest festival. Kite-flying on this day is a special feature enjoyed by both young and old. The sky is dotted with colourful kites. People also offer daan (donations) to the poor and visit temples.

Til and wheat preparations are especially made on Makar Sakranti in different parts of northern and western India. Til is a rich source of calcium, iron, protein and fat.

Festive Fare

Khana Teej Tyohar Ka

$\mathscr{T}$il laddoo
Sweet sesame balls

makes **10-12 laddoos**
preparation time **5 minutes**
cooking time **10 minutes**

Ingredients
Til (white) ○ 100g
Jaggery ○ 80g
Ghee ○ 5g

Method
- Roast til on medium flame. When til seeds puff up and start giving out a typical smell and can be easily pressed, it indicates that the til is roasted well.

- Heat ghee in a kadhai (wok), add jaggery and cook till it is melted. Keep stirring. Add roasted til and mix well to form a semi-solid sticky paste.
- Make laddoos while the mixture is hot by applying water on palms to avoid the stickiness.

Value addition
- Mawa (dehydrated milk) can be added to til laddoo.

Nutritive value

Protein g	Energy kcal	Calcium mg	Iron mg	Carotene µg	Thiamin (B1) mg	Riboflavin (B2) mg	Niacin (B3) mg
18.6	914	1544	11.3	90	1.0	0.3	4.4

Til barfi
Sweet sesame squares

makes **12 pieces**
preparation time **5 minutes**
cooking time **10 minutes**

Ingredients
Til • 100g
Mawa • 100g
Castor sugar • 100g

Method
- Roast til and grind in grinder.
- Saute mawa for 4 to 5 minutes on slow flame. Turn off the gas.
- Add the castor sugar and ground til in the mawa and mix well. Grease a flat plate and set the mixture in it. Level the mixture with a spatula.
- When the mixture is cool, cut square pieces and serve delicious and nutritive dish.

Variation
- Laddoos can be prepared from this mixture.
- Coarsely ground roasted groundnut or finely chopped dry fruits can also be added to the mawa mixture.

Nutritive value

Protein g	Energy kcal	Calcium mg	Iron mg	Carotene µg	Thiamin (B1) mg	Riboflavin (B2) mg	Niacin (B3) mg
38.3	1374	2418	9.46	209	1.24	0.8	4.8

Dudhiya kheech
Wheat and milk porridge

makes **4 servings**
preparation time **20 minutes**
cooking time **30 minutes**

This is prepared on Makar Sankranti in the Mewar region of Rajasthan.

Ingredients
Debranned wheat ∘ 100g
Milk ∘ 500g
Sugar ∘ 75g
Water ∘ 400ml
Elayichi ∘ 3-4

Method
- Soak debranned wheat overnight.
- Pressure cook for 20 minutes, add milk and cook again, stirring occasionally for 15 minutes on slow fire till the mixture thickens and becomes viscous.
- Add sugar and cook for 3 minutes. Add elayichi powder.
- Serve hot or cold as per choice.

Nutritive value

Protein g	Energy kcal	Calcium mg	Iron mg	Carotene μg	Thiamin (B1) mg	Riboflavin (B2) mg	Niacin (B3) mg
27.9	979	650	6.4	329	0.7	1.2	6.0

Kesaria bhaat
Sweetened yellow rice

Kesaria Bhaat is specially prepared on Basant Panchami, which is celebrated as spring sets in. Nature is blessed with fresh blossoms. Many people worship goddess Saraswati (goddess of learning and music) on this day.

makes **4 servings**
preparation time **5 minutes**
cooking time **20 minutes**

Ingredients

Rice ∘ 100g
Ghee ∘ 15g
Sugar ∘ 80g
Kesar (saffron/zafraan)
  ∘ 15-20 flakes
Elayichi ∘ 2 pcs
Almonds (badam) ∘ 5 pcs
Water ∘ 200ml

Method

• Wash rice and soak for 15 minutes. Heat ghee and add the rice.
• Sauté rice for 2-3 minutes. Add water and cook on slow flame till done.
• Soak kesar flakes in warm water and crush flakes.
• Add sugar and kesar water, mix well. Cook it on slow flame for 7-8 minutes.
• Garnish with elayichi powder and badam slivers and serve hot.

Nutritive value

Protein g	Energy kcal	Calcium mg	Iron mg	Carotene µg	Thiamin (B1) mg	Riboflavin (B2) mg	Niacin (B3) mg
8.9	864	42.6	1.2	90	0.1	0.1	2.34

Sheetla Ashtami is celebrated after Holi in the northern and western parts of India. It signifies the onset of summer. In Rajasthan it is one of the important celebrations both in rural and urban areas. Women dress in colourful traditional outfits. They visit temples in the morning, worship and offer prayers for the long life of their children. A variety of food items like oliya, gulgule, puri, sabzi are prepared a day in advance and is consumed on Sheetala Ashtami. This food is called *basoda* (food cooked a day before). Fresh food is not cooked on this day.

Namkeen oliya
Savoury curd rice

Plain rice is cooked a day in advance as there is no cooking to be done on the day of the festival. There is no 'cooking' involved in this dish, except the plain rice, which is mixed with other ingredients.

makes **2 servings**
preparation time **10 minutes**

Ingredients
Soft cooked rice ∘ 100g
Curd ∘ 250g
Roasted cumin
   (jeera) powder ∘ 10g
Roasted mustard
   (rai) powder ∘ 5g

Method

- Prepare hung curd by placing the required amount of curd on a muslin cloth, tying up the two loose ends of the cloth tightly to make a small sack full of curd and hanging it for ½ an hour to drain off some of its liquid (whey) from it. This makes curd less sour, thicker, smoother and more tasty. Fresh curd can also be used without draining off its water/ liquid.
- Scoop out the curd in a bowl.
- Mix cooked rice with curd.
- Add salt, roasted rai (mustard) and jeera (cumin) powder and serve at room temperature.

Nutritive value

Protein g	Energy kcal	Calcium mg	Iron mg	Carotene µg	Thiamin (B1) mg	Riboflavin (B2) mg	Niacin (B3) mg
14.1	357	456	1.37	108.5	1.4	0.49	1.53

$\mathcal{M}$eethi oliya
Sweetened curd rice

makes **6 servings**
preparation time **10 minutes**

Plain rice is cooked a day in advance as there is no cooking to be done on the day of the festival.

Ingredients
Soft cooked rice ∘ 100g
Curd ∘ 250g
Castor sugar ∘ 50g
Badam (almonds) and pista
   (pistachio) slivers ∘ 10g
Elayichi powder ∘ a pinch
Saffron ∘ a few strands

Method
- Tie curd in a muslin cloth and hang it for ½ an hour to drain off some of its liquid (whey) from it (*see the recipe on p. 127*). This makes curd less sour and adds to the taste and texture, making the curd creamy.
- Scoop out the curd in a bowl.
- Rub the saffron into one tea spoon of warm milk.
- Mix together the curd, rice, sugar, saffron mixture and elayichi powder.
- Garnish with badam (almonds) and pista (pistachio) slivers and serve at room temperature.

Nutritive value

Protein g	Energy kcal	Calcium mg	Iron mg	Carotene µg	Thiamin (B1) mg	Riboflavin (B2) mg	Niacin (B3) mg
14.2	587.5	406.5	1.35	84.7	1.4	0.5	1.69

Meethi (sweet) and namkeen (salty) papadi are made during Gangaur festival which is celebrated in the months of March-April. It is celebrated for the longevity of the husband's life. Women keep a fast and dress in colourful clothes. A procession of Gangaur Mata is taken out where women carry idols of goddess Parvati and Lord Shiva. A variety of delicacies is prepared on this occasion.

$\mathcal{M}$eethi papadi
Sweet crunchy discs

makes **10 to 12 papadi**
preparation time **10 minutes**
cooking time **15 minutes**

Ingredients
Wheat flour • 100g
Jaggery • 50g
Til seeds • 10g
Oil for moyan • 20g
Oil • for deep frying

Method
- Mix oil and til in the flour and rub it well. Dissolve jaggery in a small quantity of warm water. Add jaggery water into the flour gradually and prepare hard dough. Knead the dough well and keep it for 10 minutes.
- Make small balls and roll out each ball in 2" to 3" diameter. Prick rolled papadi with fork to avoid puffing during deep frying.
- Heat oil, fry papadi on slow fire till they turn golden. Store in air-tight container when cool.

Nutritive value

Protein g	Energy kcal	Calcium mg	Iron mg	Carotene µg	Thiamin (B1) mg	Riboflavin (B2) mg	Niacin (B3) mg
14.13	1038	233	7.15	35	0.6	0.2	4.74

Namkeen besan papadi
Savoury crisp discs

makes **10–12 papadi**
preparation time **10 minutes**
cooking time **20 minutes**

Ingredients

Besan (Bengal gram
   daal flour) • 100g
White/ all-purpose
   flour (maida) • 20g
Oil for moyan • 25g
Red chilli powder • to taste
Carom (ajwain) • a pinch
Oil • for deep frying
Salt • to taste

Method

- Mix gram flour and white all-purpose (refined) flour. Add salt, carom seeds and oil in this mixture, mix well. Prepare dough of medium hardness. Keep dough for ½ an hour.
- Make small balls and roll out in 2"-3" diameter. Prick each papadi with a fork to avoid puffing during deep frying. Heat oil and deep fry till golden.
- Store papadi in-air tight container when cool.

Nutritive value

Protein g	Energy kcal	Calcium mg	Iron mg	Carotene µg	Thiamin (B1) mg	Riboflavin (B2) mg	Niacin (B3) mg
23.0	981	60.6	5.8	134	0.5	0.2	2.9

Rabdi ke malpua
Sweet waffle

Hariyali Amavasya is celebrated in monsoon in the month of Sravan (middle of July to middle of August) to enjoy the freshness and lush greenery of the rainy season. It is a famous festival in Udaipur. A two-day mela (fair) is organised around the Fatehsagar lake and the royal Sahelio ki Bari garden resort. The first day is open to all while the second day is open only for women. Special dishes are prepared to mark the occasion. Malpua is a special preparation for this festival.

makes **20**
preparation time **15 minutes**
cooking time **30 minutes**

Ingredients

Milk • 500g
Mawa • 250g
Refined flour (maida) • 150g
Sugar • 250g
Ghee • for deep frying

Method

- Mix mawa and maida in warm milk. Beat well to avoid lumps. Strain it through steel strainer. Keep mixture of a pouring consistency.
- Make sugar syrup of half thread consistency.
- Heat ghee in a flat kadhai (wok) or a flat non-stick frying pan for deep frying the malpuas.
- Pour small quantities of batter into the hot ghee in 2 to 3 spots. When the batter fluffs up and malpuas rise, turn sides. Deep fry till golden.
- Strain out malpuas, dip in sugar syrup.
- When nicely coated with syrup, take out and drain extra syrup by pressing between two spatulas.
- Serve hot.

Nutritive value

Protein g	Energy kcal	Calcium mg	Iron mg	Carotene µg	Thiamin (B1) mg	Riboflavin (B2) mg	Niacin (B3) mg	Vit.C mg
82.8	4433	3061	5.5	765	1.0	2.0	5.1	15

oth
Festival savoury

makes **2 pieces**
preparation time **10 minutes**
cooking time **20 minutes**

Roth is prepared on Teej
and Anant Chaturdashi
festival, mainly in Jaipur
and surrounding areas. These
festivals are celebrated in the
rainy season and fall in the
months of August-September.

Ingredients

Wheat flour • 200g
Oil for moyan • 30g
Ghee • 40g
Coconut powder • 10g
Carom (ajwain) • 5g
Salt • to taste

Method

- Mix oil, salt, carom and coconut powder in flour and rub well. Make hard dough by adding water. Leave it for ½ an hour. Divide dough in two parts and make two balls.
- Roll out each ball of 1 cm thickness. Bake these roths from both the sides on slow fire. Remove from fire when it turns brown, and is done. Prick roth with knife or fork and apply ghee.
- Serve hot with raita, sabzi, pickle or ker sangri.

Nutritive value

Protein g	Energy kcal	Calcium mg	Iron mg	Carotene µg	Thiamin (B1) mg	Riboflavin (B2) mg	Niacin (B3) mg
24.9	1396	212	5.4	298	0.98	0.34	9.0

Guna
Crispy-fried sweet rings

makes **12-15 rings**
preparation time **20 minutes**
cooking time **15 minutes**

Guna is prepared
on the Ganguar
festival which
follows Holi.

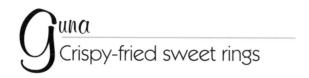

Ingredients
Maida • 100g
Sugar • 100g
Oil for moyan • 30g
Oil • for deep frying

Method
- Mix oil in flour and rub well. Make hard dough. Keep it for 15 minutes.
- Make a ball and roll it of 1 mm thickness. Cut into strips of ½" width. From each strip make round rings. Each ring can be of 1" to 2" diameter. Deep fry these rings till golden.
- Make syrup of 1½ thread consistency. Dip the fried rings in the syrup for 2 to 3 minutes. Turn the rings after a while. Finally strain out the rings from the syrup. These are called gunas.

Nutritive value

Protein g	Energy kcal	Calcium mg	Iron mg	Carotene µg	Thiamin (B1) mg	Riboflavin (B2) mg	Niacin (B3) mg
11.0	1284	23	2.7	25	0.1	0.1	2.4

Glossary

Achaar	Pickle	Garam masala	Powder of clove, black pepper, cinnamon, bay leaves, cardamom
Adarak	Ginger		
Amchur	Dry raw mango powder		
Aam ras	Ripe mango juice	Gajar	Carrot
Anaj	Cereals		
Ajwain	Carom/ Omum	Haldi	Turmeric
Atta	Unrefined wheat flour	Hamamdasta	Iron motar-pestle
Badam	Almond	Heeng	Asafoetida
Bafla	Boiled and baked/fried batis		
Bajra	Pearl millet	Imli	Tamarind
Bhaat	Rice		
Besan	Bengal gram daal flour	Jali	Flat mesh
		Jeera	Cumin seeds
Chawal	Rice	Jowar	Sorghum
Chhilka	Peels	Jou	Barley
Dana methi	Fenugreek seeds	Kali mirch	Black pepper
Daal	Broken pulse	Katori	Bowl with flat surface
Dalia	Broken cereal	Ker, sangri	Dried vegetables
Dhania	Dry coriander powder	Kesar	Saffron
Dhundharu	Smoky	Keema	Minced meat
		Kheer	Milk and rice pudding
Elayichi	Cardamom	Khoya	Condensed milk

Khana	Food	Parat	Large metal flat plate with raised edge
Kishmish	Raisin	Pista	Pistachio
Lahsan	Garlic	Ratalu	Ordinary yam
Lal mirch	Red chilly		
Laung	Clove	Saadi	Simple
Leelva	Tender green chana	Sabziyan	Vegetables
		Sabut lal mirch	Whole red chilli
Manuhar	Hospitality	Suji	Wheat rawa/ semolina
Maans	Mutton	Saunf	Fennel
Maansahari	Non-vegetarian food	Swadbhari	Full of taste
Maida	Refined/ white wheat flour		
Mawa	Condensed milk	Talwan	Deep fried
Meetha neem	Curry leaves/ kari patta	Thali	Flat big plate
Meetha	Sweet	Tej patta	Bay leaf
Methi dana	Dried fenugreek seeds	Til	Gingelly/ sesame seeds
Muli	Radish	Tikia	Flat round cutlet
Muthia	Fist shaped ball	Teej-Tyohar	Festival
Moyan	Fat added in flour as softening agent before kneading	Zaika	Taste
Padharo mahre desh	Welcome to my country/ state		

*A*ppendix

Table1. Nutritive value of commonly consumed cereals

Nutrient/100 gram	Maize dry	Maize tender	Wheat	Bajra	Jowar	Barley	Rice
Protein g	11.1	4.7	11.8	11.6	10.4	11.5	6.8
Fat g	3.6	0.9	1.5	5.0	1.9	1.3	0.5
Carbohydrate g	66.2	24.6	71.2	67.5	72.6	69.6	78.2
Energy kcal	342	125	346	361	349	336	345
Fibre g	2.7	1.9	1.2	1.2	1.6	3.9	0.2
Calcium mg	10	9	41	42	31	26	10
Phosphorous mg	348	121	306	296	290	215	160
Iron mg	2.3	1.1	5.3	8.0	2.8	1.67	0.7
Carotene µg	90	32	64	132	47	10	0
Thiamin (B1) mg	0.42	0.11	0.45	0.33	0.37	0.47	0.06
Riboflavin (B2) mg	0.10	0.17	0.17	0.25	0.13	0.20	0.06
Niacin (B3) mg	1.8	0.6	5.5	2.3	3.1	5.4	1.9

Table 2. Nutritive value of commonly consumed pulses

Nutrients/100 gram	Bengal gram daal	Black gram daal	Cowpea	Green gram whole	Green gram daal	Moth
Protein g	20.8	24.0	24.1	24.5	24.5	23.6
Fat g	5.6	1.4	1.0	1.3	1.2	1.1
Carbohydrates g	59.8	59.6	54.5	56.7	59.9	56.5
Energy kcal	372	347	323	338	348	330
Fibre g	1.2	0.9	3.8	4.1	0.8	4.0
Calcium mg	56	154	124	75	75	202
Phosphorous mg	331	385	326	326	405	330
Iron mg	5.3	3.8	4.4	4.4	3.9	9.5
Carotene µg	129	38	12	94	49	9
Thiamin (B1) mg	0.48	0.42	0.51	0.47	0.47	0.45
Riboflavin (B2) mg	0.18	0.20	0.20	0.27	0.21	0.09
Niacin (B3) mg	2.8	2.0	1.3	2.1	2.4	1.5

Table 3. Nutritive value of select vegetables

Nutrients per 100 gram

Items	Protein g	Carotene	Vit.C mg	Energy K cal	Fibre g	Cal mg	Phos. mg	Iron mg
Bathua leaves	3.7	1740	35	30	0.8	150	80	4.2
Coriander leaves	3.3	6918	135	44	1.2	184	71	1.42
Fenugreek leaves	4.4	2340	52	49	1.1	395	51	1.93
Spinach	2.0	5580	28	26	0.6	73	21	1.14
Ratalu (root vegetable)	1.4	78	Nil	111	1.0	35	20	1.19
Potato	1.6	24	17	97	0.4	10	40	0.5
Tomato	0.9	351	27	20	0.8	48	20	0.64
Green chillies	2.9	175	111	29	6.8	30	80	4.4
Garlic	6.3	Nil	13	145	0.8	30	310	1.2
Onion	1.8	15	11	59	0.6	46.9	60	1.2
Lemon	1.0	9	0	39	1.7	70	10	0.26

Turmeric/ haldi	6.3	30	Nil	349	2.6	150	28.2	6.78
Ginger	2.3	40	6	67	2.4	20	60	3.5
Peas	7.2	83	9	93	4.0	20	139	1.5
Amla	0.5	9	600	58	3.4	50	20	1.2

Table 4. Nutritive value of milk & milk products consumed in Rajasthan

Nutrients per 100 gram

Item	Protein g	Fat g	Carb. g	Energy k Cal	Cal. mg	Phos. mg	Iron mg
Milk Buffalo	4.3	6.5	5.0	117	210	130	0.2
Milk Cow	3.2	4.1	4.4	67	120	90	0.2
Curd Cow milk	3.1	4.0	3.0	60	149	93	0.2
Buttermilk	0.8	1.1	0.5	15	30	30	0.1
Khoya	14.6	31.2	20.5	421	650	420	5.8

Table 5. Nutritive value of non-vegetarian foods consumed in Rasjasthan

Nutrients per 100 gram

Item	Protein g	Fat g	Carbo. g	Energy kcal	Carotene µg	Calcium mg	Phosph. mg	Iron mg
Chicken	25.9	0.6	Nil	109	Nil	25	245	-
Mutton	18.5	13.3	-	194	9	150	150	2.5
Katla fish	19.5	2.4	2.9	111	Nil	530	235	0.9
Rohu fish	16.6	1.4	4.4	97	Nil	650	175	1.0
Egg (hen)	13.5	13.7	0.8	181	420	70	173	2.1

Table 6. Nutritive value of spices used in Rajasthan

Nutrients per 100 gram

Spices	Protein g	Carbo. g	Energy kcal	Calcium mg	Phosphorus mg	Iron mg
Carom (ajwain)	17.1	24.6	363	1525	443	12.5
Cumin (jeera)	18.7	36.6	356	1080	511	11.7

Asafoetida (heeng)	4	67.8	297	690	50	39.4
Fenugreek seeds (methi dana)	26.2	44.1	333	160	370	6.5
Red chilli powder (lal mirch)	15.9	31.6	246	160	370	2.3
Turmeric (haldi)	6.3	69.4	349	150	282	67.8
Black pepper (kali mirch)	11.5	49.2	304	460	198	12.4
Clove (laung)	5.2	46	286	740	100	11.7
Cardamom (elayichi)	10.2	42.1	229	130	160	4.6

Source: Nutritive Value of Indian Foods, C. Gopalan and others, National Institute of Nutrition, Hyderabad, Edition, 2011

Table no. 7 Recommended Daily Dietary Allowances

Group Category	Category	Protein g/day	energy Kcal/day	Calcium mg/day	Iron mg/day	Carotene μ/day	Thiamin mg/day	Ribflain mg/day	Niacin mg/day	Vit. C mg/day
Man	Sedentary	60	2320	600	17	4800	1.2	1.4	16	40
	Moderate		2730				1.4	1.6	18	
	Heavy		3490				1.7	2.1	21	
Woman	Sedentary	50	1900	600	21	4800	1.0	1.1	12	40
	Moderate		2230				1.1	1.3	14	
	Heavy		2850				1.4	1.7	16	
	Pregnant	+15	+350	1200	35	6400	+0.2	+0.3	+2	60
	lactating (up to 6 months)	+25	+600		21	7600	+0.3	+0.4	+4	80
	lactating (6-12 months)	+18	+520				+0.2	+0.3	+3	80
Children	1-3 years	16.7	1060	500	9	2800	0.5	0.6	98	25
	4-6 years	20.1	1350	600	13	3200	0.7	0.8	11	40
	7-9 years	29.5	1690	600	16	3200	0.8	1	13	40
Boys	10-12 years	39.9	2190	800	21	4800	1.1	1.3	15	40
girls	10-12 years	40.4	2010		27		1.0	1.2	13	
Boys	13 15 years	54.3	2750	800	32	4800	1.4	1.6	16	40
girls	13-15 years	51.9	2330		27		1.2	1.4	14	
Boys	16-18 years	61.5	3020	800	28	4800	1.5	1.8	17	40
girls	16-18 years	55.5	2440		26		1.0	1.2	14	

Source: Dietary Allowances for Indians 2010. D.G.N.V. Brahmam, Scientist - "F;' HOD Division of community studies, National Institute of Nutrients,(I.C.M.R.) Jama-i-Osmania (P.O.), Hyderabad - 500007

Table of Measures

The metric yields of cup and weighed measures are approximately 10% greater that the imperial yields but the proportions remain the same. Therefore for successful cooking use either metric or imperial weights or measures—do not mix the two.

Imperial Weight	Metric Weight
½ oz	15 gm
1 oz	30 gm
2 oz	60 gm
3 oz	90 gm
4 oz (¼ lb)	152 gm
6 oz	185 gm
8 oz (½ lb)	250 gm
12 oz (¾ lb)	375 gm
16 oz (1lb)	500 gm
24 oz (1½ lb)	750 gm
32 oz (2 lb)	1000 gm (1kg)
3 lb	1500 gm (1½ kg)
4 lb	2000 gm (2 kg)
oz = ounce, gm = gram, lb = pound, kg = kilogram	

Imperial Liquid Measures	Cup Measures	Metric Liquid Measures
1 fl oz		30 ml
2 fl oz	¼ cup	60 ml
3 fl oz		100 ml
4 fl oz	½ cup	140 ml
5 fl oz	¾ cup	150 ml
6 fl oz	1cup	
8 fl oz	1¼ cups	250 ml
10 fl oz	1½ cups	
12 fl oz	1¾ cups	
14 fl oz	2 cups	
16 fl oz	2½ cups	500 ml
fl = fluid ounce, ml = mililitre		

Oven Temperature Guide

Oven description	Celsius (°c)	Fahrenheit (°F)	Gas Mark
Cool	100	200	¼
Very slow	120	250	½
Slow	150	300	2
Moderately slow	160	325	3
Moderate	180	350	4
Moderately hot	190	375	5
Hot	200	400	6
Very hot	230	450	8

Acknowledgements

This book is based on our personal experience and experiments in the kitchen over a period of five decades, cooking for our dear family and friends. We are grateful to a number of friends and colleagues in encouraging us to start the work, persevere with it and finally publish it.

We thank Amit Gupta for his valuable time for capturing the images of the recipes and for providing the images on different walks of Rajasthan published in this book.

We thank Kavita Bhatnagar for contributing the recipes of several non-vegetarian delicacies.

We are also very grateful to our publishers Shri Bikash Niyogi and Smt Tultul Niyogi of Niyogi Books, New Delhi for their faith in us. We thank our editor Smt Mohua Mitra for her continuous cooperation and guidance in bringing out this book and designer Nabanita Das for executing a lovely design.

Finally, we acknowledge with gratitude, the support and love of our family. They all kept us going, and this book would not have been possible without them.

Suman Bhatnagar and Pushpa Gupta
June 2015
Udaipur

Index

Note: Pages followed by *f* or *t* represent photos or tables respectively.

Agro-climatic conditions, 22–23
Aloo paratha. *See* Bharwa/aloo paratha
Anant Chaturdashi, 135
Aravalli ranges, 16, 17*f*

Badi. *See* Mangodis/badi
Bafla bati, 30
Bajra, 26, 67
    gudmudia, 71
    kheech, 68–69*f*, 69–70
    khichada, 72
Baked wheat flour balls. *See* Bati
Barfi
    bhutta, 65–66, 65*f*
    til, 121
Basoda, 125
Bati, 28, 28*f*
    ingredients, 30
    nutritive value, 30
    recipe, 29
    types of, 30 (*See also* specific types)
Bejad roti. *See* Missi/bejad roti
Besan chakki, 85*f*
    ingredients, 85

    nutritive value, 86
    recipe, 85–86
Besan gatte, 81*f*
    ingredients, 81
    nutritive value, 82
    recipe, 82
Bharwa/aloo paratha, 42*f*
    ingredients, 42
    nutritive value, 42
    recipe, 42
Bharwa besan mirch, 91*f*
    ingredients, 91
    nutritive value, 92
    recipe, 92
Bhutta. *See* Tender maize/sweet corn/bhutta
Bhutta barfi, 65*f*
    ingredients, 65
    nutritive value, 66
    recipe, 65–66
Bhutta pakodi
    ingredients, 57
    nutritive value, 58
    recipe, 57–58
Bhutta pulav, 61*f*
    ingredients, 61
    nutritive value, 62
    recipe, 62
Bhutta sabzi, 59*f*
    ingredients, 59

    nutritive value, 60
    recipe, 60
Blanching, 96
Bran, 70

Cereals, 26
    bajra, 26, 67–72
    debranning, 69
    jowar, 26
    maize, 23, 26, 47–65
    nutritive value of, 140*t*
    wheat, 23, 26, 27–46
Chakki, besan. *See* Besan chakki
Chapati. *See* Wheat flour roti
Chicken curry, 111*f*
    ingredients, 111
    nutritive value, 111
    recipe, 111
Chilli dry dip. *See* Mirchi ke tapore
Churma, 28, 28*f*, 31*f*
    ingredients, 31
    nutritive value, 31
    recipe, 31
Costumes/dresses, 21
Cuisines, local, 23–24
Curd rice
    savoury, 126–127, 126*f*
    sweetened, 128
Curry(ies)
    chicken, 111, 111*f*

dried vegetables, 96–97
egg, 112–113, 113*f*
fish, 114–115, 114*f*
green banana peel, 95
mince, with peas, 110
nuggets, 77
papad, 104
raw turmeric dry, 105
red meat, 108–109, 109*f*
sweet corn, 59–60, 59*f*
sweet-flavoured fenugreek
    seeds, 99
yam, 89–90

Daal. *See* Pulses/daal
Daal dhokli, 36*f*
    ingredients, 36
    nutritive value, 37
    recipe, 37
Dalia
    doodh, 46, 46*f*
    raab, 51–52
Dana methi papad, 100*f*
    ingredients, 100
    nutritive value, 101
    recipe, 101
Dances, 21
    Gair, 20–21*f*
Debranning, cereals, 69
Desserts
    halwa, 45, 45*f*
    jajaria, 63–64, 63*f*
    lapsi, 35, 35*f*
Dietary Allowances, 144*t*
Doodh dalia, 46*f*
    ingredients, 46
    nutritive value, 46
    recipe, 46
Dresses. *See* Costumes/dresses
Dried vegetables curry
    ingredients, 96
    recipe, 97
Dry masala, 42, 43
Dudhiya kheech. *See* Kheech,
    dudhiya

Dupper, 32*f*
    ingredients, 32
    nutritive value, 32
recipe, 32

Egg curry, 113*f*
    ingredients, 112
    nutritive value, 113
    recipe, 112

Fast food, impact on Rajasthani
    food, 24
Fenugreek seeds
    dried, curry with papad,
        100–101
    sweet-flavoured curry, 99
Festivals
    Anant Chaturdashi, 135
    foods (*See* Foods. festivals)
    Gangaur, 18–19*f*, 129
    Hariyali Amavasya, 133
    Makar Sakranti, 117
    Sheetla Ashtami, 125
    Teej, 135
Fish curry, 114*f*
    ingredients, 114
    nutritive value, 115
    recipe, 115
Fish fry, 116*f*
    ingredients, 116
    nutritive value, 116
    recipe, 116
Foods, festivals
    dudhiya kheech, 122–123*f*
    guna, 136, 137*f*
    kesaria bhaat, 124, 124*f*
    oliya (*See* Oliya)
    roth, 134–135, 134*f*, 135*f*
    til laddoo, 118–119*f*, 119–120
Fried sweet balls. *See* Gulgule

Gair (folk dance), 20–21*f*
Gangaur festival, 18–19*f*, 129
Garlic chutney. *See* Lahsan/garlic
    chutney

Gatte, besan. *See* Besan gatte
Geographic location, 16
Ghughari, wheat, 38*f*
    ingredients, 38
    nutritive value, 38
    recipe, 38
Green banana peel curry. *See*
    Kachha kela chhilka sabzi
Green masala, 42, 43
Gudmudia, bajra
    ingredients, 71
    nutritive value, 71
    recipe, 71
Gulgule
    ingredients, 34
    nutritive value, 34
    recipe, 34
Guna
    ingredients, 136, 137*f*
    nutritive value, 136
    recipe, 136

Halwa, 45*f*
    ingredients, 45
    nutritive value, 45
    recipe, 45
Hariyali Amavasya, 133

Jajaria, 63*f*
    ingredients, 63
    nutritive value, 64
    recipe, 64
Jowar, 26

Kachha kela chhilka sabzi, 95*f*
    ingredients, 95
    recipe, 95
Kacchi haldi ki sabzi
    ingredients, 105
    recipe, 105
Kadhi pakodi, 78*f*
    ingredients, 78
    nutritive value, 79
    recipe, 78–79
Kedgeree. *See* Kheech, bajra;
    Khichada, bajra

Keema matar, 110*f*
    ingredients, 110
    nutritive value, 110
    recipe, 110
Ker sangri. *See* Pach kuta/ker
    sangri
Kesaria bhaat, 124*f*
    ingredients, 124
    nutritive value, 124
    recipe, 124
Kheech, bajra, 68–69*f*
    ingredients, 69
    nutritive value, 70
    recipe, 70
Kheech, dudhiya, 122–123*f*
    ingredients, 122
    nutritive value, 122
    recipe, 122
Khichada, bajra
    ingredients, 71
    nutritive value, 71
    recipe, 71
Khichiya, 53*f*
    ingredients, 53
    nutritive value, 54
    recipe, 53–54

Laal maans, 109*f*
    ingredients, 108
    nutritive value, 109
    recipe, 108–109
Lahsan/garlic chutney, 103*f*
    ingredients, 102
    nutritive value, 103
    recipe, 102
Lapsi, 35*f*
    ingredients, 35
    nutritive value, 35
    recipe, 35
Local cuisines, 23–24

Maize, 23, 26, 47
    makki ka dhokla, 49–50, 49*f*
    papadi/khichiya, 53–54, 53*f*
    raab, 51–52
    roti, 48, 48*f*

tender (*See* Tender maize/
    sweet corn/bhutta)
Maize roti
    ingredients, 48
    nutritive value, 48
    recipe, 48
Makar Sakranti festival, 117
Makki ka dhokla, 49*f*
    ingredients, 49
    nutritive value, 50
    recipe, 50
Malpua. *See* Rabdi ke malpua
Mangodi ki sabzi, 77*f*
    ingredients, 77
    nutritive value, 77
    recipe, 77
Mangodis/badi, 76*f*
    nutritive value, 76
    recipe, 76
Meetha/sweet paratha
    ingredients, 44
    nutritive value, 44
    recipe, 44
Meethi dana methi sabzi
    ingredients, 99
    nutritive value, 99
    recipe, 99
Meethi oliya, 128*f*
    ingredients, 128
    nutritive value, 128
    recipe, 128
Meethi papadi, 130*f*
    ingredients, 130
    nutritive value, 130
    recipe, 130
Milk/milk products
    nutritive value of, 142*t*
Milk porridge, 46, 46*f*, 122
Mince curry with peas. *See* Keema
    matar
Mirchi bada, 93*f*
    ingredients, 93
    nutritive value, 94
    recipe, 94
Mirchi ke tapore, 106*f*
    ingredients, 106

    nutritive value, 106
    recipe, 106
Missi/bejad roti
    ingredients, 33
    nutritive value, 33
    recipe, 33
Mixed daal
    ingredients, 75
    nutritive value, 75
    recipe, 75
Moth. *See* Sabut moth

Namkeen besan papadi, 131*f*
    ingredients, 131
    nutritive value, 131
    recipe, 131
Namkeen oliya, 126*f*
    ingredients, 126
    nutritive value, 127
    recipe, 127
Non vegetarian food, 107
    chicken curry, 111, 111*f*
    egg curry, 112–113, 113*f*
    fish curry, 114–115, 114*f*
    fish fry, 116, 116*f*
    keema matar, 110, 110*f*
    laal maans, 108–109, 109*f*
    nutritive value of, 142*t*
Nuggets
    curry, 77
    fried, 78–80
    sundried lentil, 76

Oliya, 125
    meethi, 128, 128*f*
    namkeen, 126–127, 126*f*

Pach kuta/ker sangri, 98*f*
    ingredients, 98
    recipe, 98
Paddy, 26
Pakodi
    bhutta, 56–57*f*, 57–58
    kadhi, 78–79, 78*f*
Pakodi sabzi
    ingredients, 80

nutritive value, 80
recipe, 80
Papadi, 129
   maize (*See* Khichiya)
   meethi, 130, 130*f*
   namkeen besan, 131, 131*f*
Papad khar, 50
Papad sabzi, 104*f*
   ingredients, 104
   nutritive value, 104
   recipe, 104
Parathas
   bharwa/aloo, 42, 42*f*
   meetha/sweet, 44
   plain, 41, 41*f*
   sabzi/vegetable, 43, 43*f*
Plain paratha, 41*f*
   ingredients, 41
   nutritive value, 41
   recipe, 41
Porridge. *See* Kheech, bajra
Pudding (halwa), 45
Pulav, bhutta. *See* Bhutta pulav
Pulses/daal, 73–74, 73*f*, 74*f*
   besan gatte, 81–82, 81*f*
   kadhi pakodi, 78–79, 78*f*
   mangodis/badi, 76–77, 76*f*, 77*f*
   mixed, 75
   nutritive value of, 141*t*
   pakodi sabzi, 80
   sabut moth, 83–84, 83*f*
Puri, 40*f*
   ingredients, 40
   nutritive value, 40
   recipe, 40

Raab
   ingredients, 51
   nutritive value, 52
   recipe, 52
Rabdi ke malpua, 132–133*f*
   ingredients, 133
   nutritive value, 133
   recipe, 133
Ratalu sabzi, 88–89*f*
   ingredients, 89

nutritive value, 90
recipe, 90
Raw turmeric dry curry. *See* Kacchi haldi ki sabzi
Red meat curry. *See* Laal maans
Regions, of Rajasthan, 18
Rice
   curd, savoury, 126–127, 126*f*
   curd, sweetened, 128, 128*f*
   sweetened yellow (*See* Kesaria bhaat)
Roth, 134*f*, 135*f*
   ingredients, 134
   nutritive value, 135
   recipe, 135
Roti
   maize, 48, 48*f*
   missi/bejad, 33
   with two layers, 32
   wheat flour, 39, 39*f*

Sabut moth, 83*f*
   ingredients, 83
   nutritive value, 84
   recipe, 84
Sabzi/vegetable parathas, 43*f*
   ingredients, 43
   nutritive value, 43
   recipe, 43
Sadi bati. *See* Bati
Savoury crisp discs. *See* Namkeen besan papadi
Savoury porridge. *See* Raab
Sheetla Ashtami, 125
Spices, 23
   nutritive value of, 142–143*t*
Stuffed bati, 30
Stuffed chillies. *See* Bharwa besan mirch
Stuffed paratha. *See* Bharwa/aloo paratha
Sweet balls
   fried (*See* Gulgule)
   wheat flour (*See* Churma)
Sweet corn. *See* Tender maize/sweet corn/bhutta

Sweet corn curry. *See* Bhutta sabzi
Sweet corn pulao. *See* Bhutta pulav
Sweet corn squares. *See* Bhutta barfi
Sweet crunchy discs. *See* Meethi papadi
Sweetened yellow rice. *See* Kesaria bhaat
Sweet paratha. ***See*** Meetha/sweet paratha
Sweet sesame balls. *See* Til laddoo
Sweet waffle. *See* Rabdi ke malpua

Talwan bati, 30
Teej, 135
Tempering process, 77
Tender maize/sweet corn/bhutta, 55
   barfi, 65–66
   jajaria, 63–64, 63*f*
   pakodi, 56–57*f*, 57–58
   pulav, 61–62
   sabzi, 59–60
Thar desert, 16
Til barfi
   ingredients, 121
   nutritive value, 121
   recipe, 121
Til laddoo, 118–119*f*
   ingredients, 119
   nutritive value, 120
   recipe, 119–120

Vegetables, 87
   bharwa besan mirch, 91–92, 91*f*
   dana methi papad, 100–101, 100*f*
   kachha kela chhilka sabzi, 95, 95*f*
   lahsan/garlic chutney, 102–103, 103*f*
   meethi dana methi sabzi, 99
   mirchi bada, 93–94, 93*f*
   mirchi ke tapore, 106, 106*f*
   nutritive value of, 141–142*t*

pach kuta/ker sangri, 98, 98*f*
ratalu sabzi, 88–89*f*, 89–90

Wheat, 23, 26, 27–46
bati, 28, 28*f*, 29–30
chapati, 39, 39*f*
churma, 28, 28*f*, 31, 31*f*
daal dhokli, 36–37, 36*f*
doodh dalia, 46, 46*f*
dupper, 32, 32*f*
ghughari, 38, 38*f*
gulgule, 34
halwa, 45, 45*f*
lapsi, 35, 35*f*
and milk porridge, 122
missi/bejad roti, 33
paratha (*See* Parathas)
puri, 40, 40*f*
Wheat flour roti, 39*f*
ingredients, 39
nutritive value, 39
recipe, 39
Whole wheat savoury. *See*
Ghughari, wheat

Yam curry. *See* Ratalu sabzi
Yellow rice, sweetened. *See* Kesaria
bhaat